The Unbowed Head

EVENTS AT SUMMERHILL ACADEMY 1968-74

by R. F. MACKENZIE, FORMER HEADMASTER

FOREWORD BY HARRY REID

E.U.S.P.B., 1 Buccleuch Place, Edinburgh, EH8 9LW.
031-667 5718

Cover design by
Jim Hutchison

Contents

To the teachers and town councillors
who supported me at Summerhill

Foreword

The time: 4 p.m. on Monday April 1, 1974. The place: the chambers of Aberdeen Corporation. The education convener, Councillor Roy Pirie, turned to to R. F. Mackenzie and said: "I have to inform you that as of now you are suspended".

Thus ended what was at once the most controversial and most celebrated headmastership Scotland has ever known. It was a moment charged with the most intense emotion. I and other journalists had just witnessed what was not so much a special meeting of Aberdeen Education Committee called to discuss the position of the headmaster of Summerhill Academy as a trial of the whole idea of the comprehensive school. That very point was made by R. F. Mackenzie in his peroration.

"It is the comprehensive school that is on trial today", he said. He went on to speak of children with wounds in their souls. "We could cure them, we could have cured them, but we were not allowed to, Mr Chairman, because you have given us a divided staff".

Mr Mackenzie's words were of no avail. The committee suspended him. The decision was taken by 16 votes to 6. Later he received a remarkably sympathetic Press. One of my colleagues, John Pirie, introduced his story with this sentence: "I accuse Aberdeen Education Committee of treachery". These were unusually emotive words with which to start a newspaper report but then it had been an unusually emotive occasion.

Mr Mackenzie had in effect been suspended because a group of parents and, more significantly, a faction of his own staff, had objected to his policies.

There were side issues and there were more detailed arguments about documents and memoranda and reports and all the minutiae of a bureaucratic dispute but at the end of the day the charge against Mr Mackenzie was best summed up by Councillor Pirie:

"Mr Mackenzie in my opinion is unwilling or unable to exercise authoritative control over his staff and secure the effective implementation of his policy, and he shows an apparent disregard for the need to win the confidence and co-operation of his staff".

Well, it was then and still is my chosen opinion that the education authority should have backed their headmaster - after all, they had appointed him in full awareness of his views - against the faction of his staff who would not support him.

Nevertheless, to be fair to Councillor Pirie, he spoke well and even movingly in deploying his case. He made a sincere speech. Equally impressive speeches were made by two of Mr Mackenzie's supporters, Councillor Bob Middleton and Mr Andrew Walls.

Mr Mackenzie heard none of these arguments and speeches; as he recalls in this book, he sat outside, in an ante-room. But as the debate reached its climax he was called in to address the committee. As he said, it was a trial. The fatal verdict came; the judgment was passed; and the next day, judge and jury were accused of treachery and the pupils of Summerhill went on strike in protest.

On the Monday evening I visited Mr Mackenzie in his farmhouse by the River Dee. A certain phrase Councillor Pirie had used earlier in the day kept insinuating itself in my mind: "The man is at the most critical point in his career - and yet he talks in parables".

The term parables had unavoidable Biblical connotations. Mr Mackenzie is himself much given to quoting from the Bible. It is pleasant to recall now how that night I gradually realised that for the first time in my life I was in the presence of someone of genuine vision: a prophet. Earlier in the day Mr Mackenzie had been accused of the "grossest arrogance" and no doubt most great prophets are sometimes arrogant in the certainty of their vision.

But that night Mr Mackenzie discarded arrogance and spoke very gently. He talked in the soft Aberdeenshire accent he has never lost; he spoke of his parents and the sacrifices they had made for his own education, an education he had come to regard as worthless; he spoke of his own children; he spoke of the tyranny of examiners; he spoke of his love and care for young people; he referred to his favourite parable, that of the lost sheep. Above all, he talked of his new book, which even then was beginning to take shape in his mind.

I remember writing the next day that no doubt this book would be subjected to the scrutiny of parents, teachers and councillors. "But they cannot suspend a book", I wrote. Well, here is that book at last.

Almost three years have elapsed since that spring afternoon in Aberdeen. I think it is reasonable to suggest that the publication of this book is the most significant event in Scottish education since R. F. Mackenzie's suspension.

The suspension was a defeat, if a temporary one. The publication of this book is a permanent victory. Talking to R. F. Mackenzie that evening in 1974, I realised for the first time that it was not children who most needed education, but parents and indeed all adults. This book will not only regale and amuse and enlighten and entertain; it will also educate.

Harry Reid,

Education Correspondent, "The Scotsman"

Chapter One

CRISIS IN THE CLASSROOM

"A gaunt and arid intellectualism". That was how one of Scotland's most distinguished teachers, Sir James Robertson of the Aberdeen Grammar School, described Scottish education. This book is the story of an attempt to bring a more humane attitude into the tawse-controlled classrooms of Scotland.

I know now that the Summerhill experiment was never on. Somebody recently said that the great mistake we educationists make is to suppose that schools are about education. It is not so, he said; schools are about control.

When we started at Summerhill in 1968 the administrators were still confident that they could contain the pressures, and were prepared to support some experimental work in education. When the experiment was terminated in 1974 it was because they were alarmed and saw the school as a threat to their system of government and control.Since then the crisis in our society has deepened. Watergate and Lockheed and Lonrho have cracked the propaganda bell and in our lifetime it will never ring so wooingly again. Colour television brought the goon shows of American presidential conventions and the nightmare landscape of Seveso, Northern Italy into millions of homes. The impact on many people, school educated to believe in the organisers of democracy, was as if a humble mediaeval believer had been privileged to view intimately a day and a night in the life of a Borgia pope. The corruption of politics in the north-east of England, the story of thalidomide and of asbestos, the immunity of the British industrialists who broke the sanctions against Rhodesia; these things have stimulated enquiry. It doesn't need a special gift of prophecy to foresee that there are going to be more such stories, more vandalism of the atmosphere and the countryside, more juvenile delinquency and more urgent campaigns against juvenile delinquency, more erosion of trust in the politicians and administrators. The campaigns will be largely unproductive. Their desperate efforts to have it both ways are doomed to failure. They spend tens of thousands of pounds on reducing alcoholism while supporting a system which spends many millions advertising to increase it. In these circumstances they are little disposed to further experimental work in education. The educational landscape is darker than it was in 1968. The crisis in Scottish schools is a crisis in Scottish life. The EUSPB yearbook of Scottish government 1976-77 began, "Scotland is a perplexing place". Scotland's schools are at the centre of Scotland's perplexity, one of its main causes. They make little contribution to its cultural development, they are insulated from dealing with the problems of ordinary life. In their uniforms, discipline, and discouragement of original thought they are authoritarian like the army but even more rigid than the army, which no longer flogs its recalcitrants. The democracy of Scottish education (and Scottish life) is a myth. Proportionately fewer Scottish working-class children go to the university now than fifty years ago. Comprehensive education made tragically little impact on this tradition. Labour MPs are content to leave the work that goes on in the schools largely as it is. They are indifferent to the sense of rejection which that means for the majority of Scottish youngsters. I sympathise with Father Anthony Ross who wrote in the Year Book that 'For a long time most Catholics in Scotland were second class citizens. That is one historical reason for the defence of a special school system cherished by the community too many of whose members have been faced with the choice of Protestantism or hunger, in the nineteenth century and even more recently. For integration to become a reality there must be deeper self-criticism on the part of many Scottish Protestants' . But the Catholic children aren't the only children who are rejected. The cleavage within the state schools is as deep; and integration as dependent on a deeper self-criticism on the part of the education committees. It is the education committees who have lit the fire in the bellies of the young.

This book is addressed to the problem of what we do to make a vital change in Scottish education so that we can integrate our pupils (and therefore our society) . It's more difficult now than it would have been in 1968. Attitudes have hardened, distrust is deeper. The white settlers of Rhodesia aren't the only governing body whose obituary will be ''Too little and too late''. Scotland's schools, inflexible, lacking in self-criticism, always with an assumption of righteous indignation blaming the pupils, unable to adapt themselves to new circumstances of living, may go the way of the dinosaurs and be replaced by a totally different way of bringing up children, more flexible, more nimble-minded, kindlier. What is new in our society is the dawning realisation that all human systems and modes of association are now accessible to enquiry and may be replaced. Nothing is sacrosanct. The framework of Scottish society is up for a major overhaul.

But that wasn't as clear in 1968 as it is now. At Summerhill we settled for a more modest experiment. We still thought in terms of a crisis in the classroom, and that we could solve it in the classroom. We wanted to humanise the school, making it a friendly, family place where all the children were of equal concern to us and where they could increase in understanding and happiness. We knew that the abilities of most children, physical, intellectual, creative, had been underestimated. We thought it would be possible to harmonise all that power within the school. I thought of Sagres, the Portuguese seaport at the time of Henry the Navigator where sailors and workmen experimented with compasses, astro-navigation, building different kinds of ships, making trial runs, learning, discussing, always preparing for those voyages of exploration down the long African coast and across the Atlantic. I thought of education in the twentieth century as comparable to exploration in the fifteenth, a sphere of activity making its own discoveries.

Part of the cause of the crisis in the classroom is a failure of communication. Somebody estimated that three quarters of what the teachers say is not understood by the pupils. That's partly due to the fact that when we have completed an argument about current affairs over our morning coffee we leave the staffroom and continue the discussion in the classroom in the same idiom, forgetting that the pupils have a more restricted vocabulary. But it is also due to the abstract nature of most textbooks and political and social discussion. It is an excellent classroom exercise to take a politician's speech and reduce the abstract terms into the concrete details which he may have in mind. Sometimes it is an impossible exercise and the pupil thinks it is his or her fault in not having the necessary intelligence to understand the abstract terms; but frequently it is the politician's fault because his speech was waffle, abstraction unrelated to anything in real life. This kind of abstraction, defeating the majority of children, diminishes their confidence and makes them feel they are unsuited to serious political or philosophical discussion. Some teachers deify the abstractions, believing that it is "the capacity for abstract thought" that differentiates intelligent ("academic") pupils from the majority. I think the phrase "capacity for abstract thought" is imprecise and needs analysis. Sometimes it is only the ability to be conned by abstract words. At school and university I became good at manipulating abstract terms, giving the impression that I understood what I was saying. But I didn't. Our pupils need to be sustained by honesty and clarity of expression, and they crave for it.

We should teach our pupils always to refer an abstraction back to the concrete reality of which the abstract term is only a portmanteau. It is a salutary and sometimes an amusing exercise. In **I, Claudius,** the Emperor, Augustus is flattered to be deified by the people of Palmyra but realistic enough to say, "They will pray to me to be cured of their gout. But how can I cure them of their gout?'' That's the kind of reference back to reality that our education system lacks. Much of the history taught in school is kept under these abstract wraps.

When encouraged by emphasis on clear, concrete thinking,children have more intellectual ability and subtler powers of discrimination than it has suited the education departments to recognise. Many of the heads of these departments are not up to the rigours of the kind of analysis of their thinking that such a training would develop among the young. We have much to learn from our children, the simplicity and directness of their thinking, their blunt honesty. They have also sensitivity, an instinctive judgement, trust and human kindness, they are less self-regarding than most adults and they have a more vivid imagination. Jesus of Nazareth and Blake and Wordsworth and many other teachers said all that in a less prosaic way and they meant it literally. But our brutal Scottish schools crush the offering that the children bring to the classroom. What makes the spectacle more zombie-like is that most of the people who do the crushing are not themselves brutal. It is as if they had surrendered control of their thinking and were responding to messages subtly communicated to them from outside. The Americans conducted an official enquiry into their university and school systems and it was published in book form under the title of **Crisis in the Classroom.** In a review the **New York Times** summarised the findings of the enquiry by quotations from the book. It said that ''America's schools destroy spontaneity and joy and fail to educate. . . . What's wrong has much less to do with technique or substance than with the mindlessness of the whole enterprise. Nobody's encouraged to think about the purpose of his work, why he's doing what he does. . . . The way public schools are organised destroys spontaneity, initiative, and love of learning among teachers as well as students. . . . The public schools are quite literally destructive of human beings. I think they are the most grim, joyless places on the face of the earth. They are needlessly authoritarian and repressive — not because teachers and principles are stupid or venal, but because nobody ever asks why: why the rules, or why the curriculum?''

Scotland's complacent educationists in universities and colleges of education, trade unions, education committees and Parliament would be well advised to read this book. The Scottish schools share with the American schools this mindlessness, this lack of curiosity, the discouragement of questions.

I asked a seventeen year old pupil to tell me about the science he did in school and this is what he wrote.

''Capacitors, inductors, alternative current, oscillating current. We learned about these things but never what they are used for. Why do we have to do this? 'It's to get your Highers and a good job', we're often told. I could do the theory and the equations but I was puzzled about how this fitted into life. I've begun to understand it now but it wasn't at the school that I learned; it was at the local electrician's. My friends and I were preparing for a hop that night. We needed to wire up a circuit with six switches to take two 100 watt amplifiers, a light switch, a record player and two switches for anything extra. A friend and I went to the electrician's.

'Twelve feet of cable and six sockets please,' I asked.

'What amperage and what kind of wire, heavy duty?'

'I'm sorry; I'm afraid I have no idea', I said.

'Well, what is it being used for and we can see?'

I told him and from that he totalled up the current that the flex would have to carry.

'This will do; the wire and sockets will both take the current. Do you know how to fix it up? And don't forget the new colour code'.

'No, I don't know the new colour code', I said, 'but I can fix it up; break the wire in five places and then join up the plugs'.

That isn't the best way; that way you're losing a little current each time because of loose bits of wire. Look, do this. Bare the wire at each point where it is connected to each plug. The colour code - well, the blue is neutral, the striped - that's the earth, and the brown - that's the live. Okay?'

In the quarter of an hour I was in that shop I learned more of the practical use of electricity than in four years of Physics in school. Although we could do the equations in school the electricity was unintelligible, and that brought on boredom and a breakdown of the relationship between pupil and teacher. It was the same with Maths, - one huge mass of equations and proofs".

A youngster of seventeen was saying the same as the enquiry into American education which spoke of the "mindlessness' of the classroom work. They just went on doing what they had always done, and without asking any questions. It is the pupils who now ask the questions. When I was seventeen I just accepted it all; I believed.

As the seventeen year old pupil observed, Maths is a remote study. It hasn't altered much since I was at school. We learned Euler's Theorem and we were as good at manipulating mathematical symbols as Latin symbols (ablative absolute and "ut" with the subjunctive) but we never knew what the mathematical symbols symbolised and nobody explained why we studied mathematics. Nobody said what kind of man Euler was. Like Vergil, he remained in the shadows. It would have made a break if somebody had interrupted a lesson to tell us what kind of a man Ohm was and what led him to the discovery of his law and Euler to the formulation of his theorem and Vergil to the writing of his peom. Always there was the feeling that this kind of enquiry was vulgar, a trivial inquisitiveness like gossip, and we were not to be diverted from the strait and narrow path of pure scholarship by such trivialities. There wasn't a living, suffering, sinning character anywhere on the landscape; nothing but symbols, pure symbols.

The Scottish schools share with the Amrican schools a rhinoceros hide, an ability to take all the criticism and to blunder on without change of direction. In spite of the powerful reform movements in the 1950s and 1960s American schools have remained largely unchanged. In the USA technical gimmickry and different packaging had been introduced but the content of the curriculum and the process of instruction had been left untouched and, for the most part, unexamined. The curriculum was a mixture of unrelated and inane details. It was easier to put man on the moon than to reform the public schools. Educational television in the U.S.A. followed the same pattern, having little, said the report, to equal the BBC's **Culloden** an unusual production which showed what imaginative teaching could be like.

Scottish schools are the same. This year the pupils in Turriff School in Aberdeenshire are plodding through **Macbeth** in the same way as Shakespeare plays were plodded through when I was a pupil there. The American frustration is the Scottish frustration, except that no Scottish official publication has so indicted its schools as this American official publication does. And that says something about the difference between Scotland and America. I've copied out these quotations so that readers of the present book may have a background of comparison against which to measure the complacency with which Scottish education's official spokesmen reassure parents that there is no need for vital change in Scotland's schools.

Many Scottish teachers have told me of their frustration when confronted by such massive indifference. What **can** we do? they ask. I think the remoteness of the Scottish senior educationists is an inevitable result of what the American report calls "education for docility". Historical patterns repeat themselves as humanity goes round its treadmill. In the ninth century before Christ the people of Israel, like the people of Scotland nearly three thousand years later, were looking to their establishment figures to guide them, but at a largely attended meeting convened at Mount Carmel to discuss a crisis in their national life, "There was no voice nor any that answered". Then Elijah mocked them, says the Bible, and said, "Cry aloud, for he **is** a god; either he is talking, or he is pursuing, or he is on a journey, or peradvanture he sleepeth, and must be awakened". The whole livelong day they beseeched their god to help them. But "there was neither voice, nor any answer, nor any that regarded".

Establishment figures don't change much down the ages. They are forever on a journey,to committee meetings or conferences, talking. I'm not sure what Elijah meant when he said that the establishment figure 'is pursuing', but I can guess. He was busy catching up with his correspondence or his appointments; or perhaps he was off to an educational conference at Tyre or Sidon; or maybe it just wasn't convenient for him to attend this confrontation at Mount Carmel. In Scotland we are in the process of escaping from a myth about our schools. I doubt if they were ever at any time in the last hundred years as nourishing to the great majority of the people of Scotland as we were brought to believe. It is this myth, I think,which makes the educational authorities of Scotland so unresponsive. The English schools weren't all that good but they knew it and they have been trying to do something about it. The Scottish schools thought they were wonderful and did nothing. The Education Committee which interviewed me on a wintry day early in 1968 knew how I regarded Scottish education. They may have read the books in which I described how a group of us in Fife had attacked the mindlessness and indifference of the system. The Aberdeen chairman asked me what I understood by comprehensive education, thus giving me· an opportunity to spell out clearly what I'd like to do at Summerhill. When they appointed me I was in no doubt that they would give me their support and I entered the portals of Summerhill with a sober optimism.

Chapter Two

SUMMERHILL
SCHOOL

My predecessor was Summerhill's first headmaster. He was a keen Episcopalian. The Episcopalians are one of the strands that made the web of Scottish history. He was concerned to make it clear that Episcopalianism was not just a Scottish branch of the Church of England but a church in its own right, having contacts with similarly-minded people in England. In their cathedral in King Street in Aberdeen the Episcopalians worship their God with more colour and drama and people-participation than the Presbyterians do; but who shall say that their ritual is less native to the north-east than that of the greyer Church of Scotland? The morning assemblies at Summerhill took on an Episcopalian flavour but Scottish education is tolerant in this field.

The school grew and prospered. It had its troubles but these were minor. The headmaster lived for the school. He was devoted to the interests of staff and pupils. Every day he made an appearance in all the classrooms, so that his presence permeated the school. Teachers stayed on after four o'clock, in order to prepare work for the next day or tidy up loose ends or to relax in the easy chairs of the staffroom and drink coffee and chat about the day's events. Much of this esprit de corps was due to the work and outlook of my predecessor; he believed in easy relationships within a framework of discipline. He was an independent-minded man whose way of life was based on his religious beliefs. There was a stubborn honesty about him. He stood firmly within the Scottish educational tradition but wanted it to extend its benefits to far more working-class children; and that was in the Scottish democratic tradition.

He gave to the school something of the cheerful briskness that would have pleased a clean-shaven Roman centurion. Provided there was no slacking, that pupils walked smartly to their classes and paid attention when they were at their lessons, kept themselves neat and tidy, were courteous and co-operative and hard-working, they were treated with genuine friendliness and sympathy. The Education

Committee had generously furnished and equipped the school, very much supporting this new junior secondary school in its programme of (in the words of the time) 'broadening the education highway'.

My predecessor had been involved in the discussion of the initial plans and with a group of carefully chosen principal teachers and assistants he had meshed into the Scottish tradition the requirements of the Education Act which set up secondary modern schools in England and junior secondary schools in Scotland in 1944 and 1945. He had a clear idea of what the junior secondary school should be. He was very much a product and a part of the Scottish tradition. He was proud of its academic achievements, its strict discipline, in his case administered with human kindness. I told him once that when I first came to Summerhill some pupils had chatted in a friendly way over school dinner and then one of them said, "And now can I sell you a ticket for our Girl Guides' concert?" He was pleased because this is what he had hoped and laboured to achieve - this feeling of friendliness and confidence on the part of pupils who previously had been little esteemed in the Scottish elitist system. The Scottish educational tradition had been proud of its success in making a highway to the university for the children of poor parents who had proved their academic worth. He wanted to broaden the highway. He believed that far more pupils than was generally believed could benefit from an academic education. He would meet a senior pupil in a corridor and ask, "What career are you aiming at when you leave the school?" If a girl answered, "A nurse", he would ask, "Why not a doctor?" If a boy said, "A quantity surveyor", he would ask, "Why not an architect?"

I understand and support this outlook. What he was saying was that the ability of ordinary pupils has been much under-estimated. I think that that is entirely true. His purpose was to give to a much bigger number of pupils the confidence to sit the examinations and go to the university. He believed in the tradition; he wanted to give it a wider application. Thus the pupils were to be brought up in the tradition, wearing the uniform, doing their homework conscientiously, showing that Summerhill Junior Secondary pupils were every bit as good as the pupils at Aberdeen Grammar School or Aberdeen Girls' High School. A College of Education survey had identified the Summerhill parents as 'upper working class'. I know what they meant. They saw the parents as members of the ambitious section of the working class eager that their children should profit by the opportunities that had not been available to them, supporting their children and hoping that they would get the education certificates that would help them to climb some rungs of the social ladder.

But there was more to it than that. My predecessor wanted further to broaden the Scottish tradition by admitting cookery and woodwork and metalwork. making these skills respectable and acceptable in an educational system which had hitherto denied them. And these developments were within the Scottish tradition. At one time there was no professor of English Literature at Aberdeen University; English literature was a sub-section of the ruling Classics departments. But now English had been accepted as a reasonable subject capable of having its own department. Similarly, my predecessor believed Scottish education would in due course accept these subjects, cookery and technical subjects, into full and equal communion.

But the ethos of the Grammar School remained. The pupils that the Grammar School approved of and gave its cachet to (for example, in recommendations to employers) were (with these modifications) those that Summerhill approved of. They were docile, smart in appearance, neat and tidy,hard-working,co-operative,right-thinking. short-haired, uniform-wearing, concerned for the reputation of the school, good prefects. There were enough statistics to show that some pupils selected at the age of twelve ('eleven plus' in England where they moved into the secondary school a year earlier) for the Grammar School did less well than some pupils rejected and sent to the junior secondary school. This was the area within which Summerhill did good work.

He wore himself out in the interests of his pupils, and although he had not reached the age for retiral, he decided to bid farewell to the school. After an interview by the Education Committee I was appointed. Before I took up duty I was invited to visit the school. I arrived at 2 p.m. on a February afternoon, but stayed in the car outside the school to let the school settle down for the afternoon. Litter lying along the edge of the grass was blown about by the spring wind. Pupils arriving late furtively crept into the school building. I felt a sense of relief, remembering Braehead, in Fife, where there was litter and pupils arriving late. "At least these are two things I won't be blamed for", I said at the time (But I was wrong. Three years later at a Principal Teachers' meeting, a member of the staff attributed the litter and the lates to me).

The school I had come from had 500 pupils. Summerhill was much bigger and soon grew to over 1,000 pupils. I discovered that it is much more than twice as difficult to introduce changes in a school of 1,000 pupils than in a school of 500 pupils. There is a much bigger inertia to overcome. And there was the natural resistance of a staff which had co-operated happily and successfully in a policy for several years.

The staff were co-operative - and watchful. They and I were willing to give one another the benefit of the doubt, exploring the no-man's land between us. I heard of a potential enemy, a ringleader of staff, who had not got on well with my predecessor, and took him on a pub crawl and we had a pleasant evening of discussion. I was impressed by the amount of time that the great majority of the staff gave, unpaid, to help pupils' societies, practices, concerts, treks. Wisely my predecessor had united all the staff in one large staffroom of which the southern side, largely glass, looked out on the shrubbery of a large quadrangle.

Some evenings I went to watch a girls' netball team play their rivals in other city schools. They were outstanding in their maroon skirts and in their success. This was how a school builds up a reputation, and the reputation is associated with the school uniform. In swimming and in football the school was carrying off the championships. It was a junior secondary school that ambitious working class parents from the surrounding estate could take pride in. A neighbour or a cousin might have a child at one of the prestigeous schools, wearing its well-known uniform, belonging to its mystery; but Summerhill was an up-and-coming school, its attractive school uniform was being recognised, its games record blossoming, employers spoke appreciatively of its products. All this was 'recognition'. Parents basked in the reflected sunshine and no longer felt out in the cold when relatives boasted of the school that their child attended.

Visitors from overseas were directed to the school. It was one of the schools that, they were told, they ought to see. There was a very attractive swimming pool, it had the best and best provided technical department in the city, the dining hall and the school dinners were excellent. The meals really were very good, better than in several hotels, and visitors enjoyed them and the opportunity to talk to the pupils during the meal. Smartly dressed girls served coffee in the Homecraft department and occasionally came and talked to visitors. There was a friendly relationship between staff and pupils. There was a large hall which had a deep stage and a battery of lights, and above the stage was the school's coat of arms. From time to time at the morning assembly I explained to pupils what the coat of arms meant. It was surmounted by a crown and the crown could also be interpreted as a stockade. The school stood in what had been the Forest of Stocket, gifted by Robert the Bruce to the people of Aberdeen for their help at the Battle of Bannockburn. I explained to the pupils that stocket, stockade, Stockholm were all words of the same derivation which indicated the Scandinavian part of our ancestry (just as Kingsgate, the thoroughfare that comes from the centre of the city towards Summerhill, was a Scandinavian word meaning King's 'Street). Beneath the crown or stockade was a leopard (from the city's coat of arms) and in front of it a book, which indicated that we were engaged in education; and below the shield were the words 'Mak siccar'. All of them had been authenticated by the Lord Lyon and had cost the school some £40. 'Siccar', I explained, meant secure or sure. But the pupils forgot what it meant and I was never sure what it was that the motto exhorted them to make sure of, and I forgot the words like argent and gules which the Lord Lyon has used to describe the coat of arms. 'The boast of heraldry' (as it is called in Gray's **Elegy**) is a mediaeval survival, a kind of spider's web which has entangled people's thinking. It is picturesque, it is intended to provide a core, like uniforms and a gay flag, round which people will unite in a common identity. But it is an emblem of more than that; for Summerhill School it was a sign that the school accepted the tradition and was accepted by it. Like the Union Jack, it was a symbol of an Establishment which we served. Even at that time I was vaguely uneasy about it. The school was making the grade. It was **establishing** itself.

On several occasions I was invited with other headmasters to cocktail parties on board visiting frigates and submarines at the harbour. Ratings saluted us on arrival, attended us politely and the whisky flowed freely. I enjoyed the outings, and some excellent discussion with the officers. I wondered what the officers thought of us. Did they think that we were obtuse enough to believe that the entertainment was all neighbourly convivality; or did they regard it as a cold chore, a calculated exercise in public relations, to induce in us a sedated attitude to the high costs of the Fighting Services and to encourage us to act as recruiting officers?

There were two formal visits to the Town Chambers where the candelabra sparkled and glittered, and dignified portraits of Lord Provosts looked down at us. some of them knights, some decked in the uniform of senior military officers. Were they there to impress us, to show us what a dignified, noble company the establishment was officered by, and to discourage any thoughts of stepping out of line? I enjoyed the glitter of these formal occasions as I had enjoyed the spectacle of a Nazi torchlight march, with stirring music, at Dusseldorf in the snow of 1938.

The army and the navy and the air force sent recruiting officers to the school. They showed films and told the pupils what a wonderful life it was in the services; you got a technical education and you had sport and adventure and you saw the world. You could also be killed, but they didn't refer to that. Some of the pupils were keen to enlist, some of them to escape from intolerable home conditions to a set-up where there were good, regular meals and a consistent attitude on the part of authority and there were sometimes commanding officers who took a genuine interest in their welfare. I helped the pupils to fill in their forms and wrote the kind of testimonial which would make their entry easier.

These were still the easy days. Occasionally clouds hid the sun and there were some showers, but these were incidental things. The school, as they said, was in good heart. The pupils were doing well with 'O' grade passes. This examination had been introduced from England a few years earlier but to mask its English derivation the

Scottish Education Department decided to call it not the 'O' Levels but the 'O' Grades. Most parents, accustomed to the English term in television discussions, persisted in calling it the 'O' levels. In those days the school's policy was simple. It existed to get as many pupils as possible through the 'O' Grades, even in one or two subjects. An Aberdeen firm had already decided to co-operate with the educational establishment to the extent that they wouldn't employ a pupil as a joiner unless he had passed his 'O' grade in woodwork. But there were, unfortunately, pupils who were unlikely to pass any 'O' grades, pupils who, like the poor, were always with us, and since we were a Christian community it behoved us to bear with them and their inadequacies. We would treat them with kindness, provide 'remedial education' and hope to hell that when then left the school they would get the kind of job which wouldn't make too obvious the cruelty of the competitive, examination-based system which directed our lives.

Most human associations have been uneasy efforts to get a variety of people to settle down together, the lion and the lamb. Any establishment underplays its stresses; the slaves are generally well-treated and happy, it assures itself; the natives wouldn't know what to do with the money if you paid them European rates. But each civilisation contains within itself the seeds of its own decay. These seeds were already growing in the Summerhill soil before I arrived there. The staff pushed out of their consciousness the kind of lives that the factory-fodder, non 'O' grade pupils, would live; they minimised the mutterings of revolt that came from a few independent, resolute spirits who refused to bow to Baal.

"Have you met Craig Peterson yet?" a teacher would ask me when I went into the staffroom for a morning-break cup of coffee.

"No" I replied.

"You will", was the usual answer.

I did. A teacher came along with three pupils who, he said, had been grossly discourteous to him. After he left I talked to them. The spokesman explained the situation. "Well, we were going along the corridor when the teacher shouted, 'Where you going? Where you going?' We replied, "We dinna ken". If he'd said quietly, 'Where are you going?' we'd have told him". I asked him his name. "Craig Peterson", he said.

Craig had an independent streak and an immunity to establishment carrots that made him unacceptable in the school. Any authoritarian society has an allergy to these characters. In the army they are called 'bolshy', 'barrack-room lawyers', and cajoled and threatened. For centuries they persisted against all the odds, however small the minority in which they found themselves. Porcupine characters, uncomfortable and inconvenient. When I was at school we did what we were told; we feared criticism and denigration, we fought one another for promotion and preferment. Craig had different values; he was independent at whatever cost to himself, he insisted on human dignity. It's like the slaves or the suffragettes; there comes a time when you can't pretend any longer that their protests can be ignored. You have to reallocate the resources of your society so that their requirements can be met in full, - so that they can live at peace within the terms of your association. Craig Peterson was the precursor of this revolution in Summerhill.

In 1970, Craig Peterson's pioneers were merely á headache in the body of the educational system. They could be isolated and prevented from spreading the infection. They received the admiration of a large number of pupils but they could be removed from the classrooms by the provision of practical jobs round the school. I asked some of the senior staff to recommend half a dozen boys to go and tidy up the Highland lodge the school had been presented with. The Education Committee were going to visit the lodge to see if they would support us in this venture and there was three days' work sweeping and dusting and scrubbing to make the place presentable. The pupils whose names were given for this work were Craig Peterson's and five of his lieutenants; they were expendable; and teachers were relieved at their absence. They helped to sweep a chimney, dug a pit to bury rubbish, cleaned and scrubbed and hammered. It was an impressive eruption of energy and goodwill. They enjoyed, I think, both the sheer hard physical activity and the awareness of doing something of value. Years later, leaving a first division football match at Pittodrie, I met Craig. He said: "Did you ever get that Highland lodge going?" I replied, "No, the education committee wouldn't support us." He said, "Do you know, that was the best three days of my life."

Every proposed innovation caused a staff meeting controversy. Social work was not part of a school's function. A pupil's council would take prestige and power from the teachers. A school newspaper was a frivolity, diverting attention from the proper work of education.

A part time teacher of ballet was very popular with the girls whom she was instructing. I proposed that she should give more teaching time to the school. She came to me in tears because of the hostility towards her that this suggestion had provoked in the staffroom. Some teachers said that because she wan't a certificated teacher (that is, she hadn't attended a College of Education course on teaching ballet) they would resist her work at every step. The fact that there was no course on teaching ballet made no difference to their hostility.

I understood this bitter resistance. Scottish teachers have fought a long and difficult battle for recognition, and the result is still in the balance. Many of them, graduates in secondary schools, would have been doctors or lawyers if their parents' income had permitted them to take the more expensive training. Teaching has never had the prestige of medicine. The doctors have a mystery but everybody has been to a school and know what happens there. Most of the adult population remember their schooldays without enthusiasm and the teaching profession is not popular with the public. Their pay has lagged behind that of comparable groups. No section of the Scottish population has been so conscientious as the teachers. They worked in the evenings and weekend unpaid. They drove themselves as hard as they drove their pupils and sometimes met pupils' ingratitude or even enmity. When married women returned to the profession, their home and husband commitments would not permit them to stay after four in the afternoon or take games at the weekend and they opted out. The others resented the greater burden that thereby fell on their shoulders. There were increased pressures in the classroom as the school leaving age was raised, and more and more unwilling pupils broke the industrious silence. Meantime the whole Scottish education tradition and a way of life (in which they were deeply involved, being the keepers of the covenant, the official handers-on of the tradition to the next generation), was under assault. The value of the ancient learning was itself queried. They were like an established priesthood whose standing was undermined by the emergence and success of a competing faith. From all of these grievances an angry reaction began to gather pressure among Scottish teachers.

There was the same response when I proposed that there should be no belting of girls. The tawse or leather belt is an integral part of the Scottish educational tradition. A saddler at Lochgelly in Fife, surveying the decreasing part that the horse was playing in Scottish life, salvaged his business by turning out leather belts for the use of teachers in primary and secondary schools. He was interviewed in a BBC radio programme. The dead-pan interviewer asked him to describe the kind of belt that was sold to the teachers of the younger pupils in the primary schools, a small, simple piece of leather. For older pupils in the primary school a heavier belt, split into more fingers at the end, was required. And finally, for the oldest secondary pupils there was the Piece de Resistance, the masterpiece of the leather workers' art, a five fingered heavy belt.

You could say without too much exaggeration that the Scottish educational system is based on the tawse. Take it away and part of the system crumbles. What do you put in its place? many teachers ask. It is an admission that the educational system is based on punishment, depends on punishment. Dark shadows from a pre-Christian world linger in the classrooms of the twentieth century, shadows of fear. Life is a jungle and we are explorers securing our camp for the night. The natural instincts are jungle beasts and must be guarded against, like tigers or savage tribes. The idea that love casteth out fear has no currency in these circumstances.

I read the translation of an Italian novel called **Christ stopped at Eboli**. I was interested in the novel because I had cycled from Naples to Eboli and over the hills through basilicata and by way of Gravina and Altamura to Italy's east coast. The idea of the novel was that Christianity never penetrated farther in the wild pagan interior than Eboli. Beyond Eboli lay the territory that the Chicago gangsters came from. (I met one of them a refugee from Chicago, spending his retirement in his native town teaching the Italian children to swear in English. At his behest they turned on a demonstration in my honour). The idea of the novel was an eye-opener. Our education had taught us about the Christianising of Europe and then of much wider regions. For the first time somebody had articulated the thought that maybe it wasn't true. Maybe the boundaries of Christianity were much more limited than the teachers and the history books said. Maybe as far as Scotland was concerned, Christ stopped at Iona.

We had too readily accepted that because it had cathedrals and bishops and dioceses it must be Christian. More likely it remained pagan throughout two thousand years. Its dark, suspicious, villent outlook on life had survived countless attempts at conversion and similarly the spirit of the Sermon on the Mount didn't penetrate into many Scottish schools.

Few things are as unChristian as the Scottish educational system. The intense competitiveness, the intense seeking for individual gain, the carelessness about the under-dog, the hitting of young children with a leather belt belong to an older world. It's a dark, troubled psyche that broods over the Scottish classroom. We feel guilty about all this hitting of children. We say that theoretically we are against it but we justify ourselves by saying that we live in a real world and must be realistic about it. We talk significantly about 'the problem of evil', thus justifying our use of the belt. Then we raise our spirits by saying that the belt is now much less than it used to be. Then the teachers' unions throw doubt on the idea by refusing to allow teachers to keep a record of the occasions on which the belt is used.

There are three main unions of teachers in Scotland - Educational Institute of Scotland (46,000 members); the Scottish Secondary Teachers Association (7,500 members); and the Scottish Schoolmasters' Assocation (3,000 members). All of these, like any other trade union, want a better deal for their members; all of them are reactionary associations, looking to the past and unwilling to participate in vital changes in education. They are fighting all the things that make life difficult for the teachers. - Low salaries, bad working conditions, recalcitrant pupils. They want salaries to be raised, conditions to be improved and pupils to be disciplined. They look back at the golden age of Scottish education when gifted children of poor parents, the 'lads o' pairts' (like negro children in African secondary schools today), bent their heads in concentration over their Latin grammars and with the selfless help of the village dominie, the ploughman's son went to the university. Many, many youngsters who would have been excluded from the universities in England because their parents were poor, found their way to the university of Scotland, and became ministers, doctors, teachers, and senior civil servants in India. What was happening in the village classrooms when the dominie was concentrating on the lads o' pairts? That question was overlooked, and Scotland got a reputation for being a more democratic country than England. In that golden era, before the age of permissiveness, it was a pleasure for a Scottish dominie to practice his profession, a guide, philosopher and friend to the eager acolyte preparing for the academic priesthood, lending him books, gently correcting his mistakes and maintaining contact with him when he was living off a sack of oatmeal in a lodging in Aberdeen,and working through the night on translation of Ovid and Thucydides.

The Scottish teaching profession is a prisoner of that vision beatific. It is against the raising of the school leaving age because that measure, like an Aberdeen trawl net, dredged up all manner of unprofitable material. It wants to deal with the selected minority who will get on quietly with the traditonal job of absorbing knowledge. The rest, the great majority, it regards as unsuitable for continuing education although it is prepared to make a concession to the spirit of the times by providing for them a programme of handwork and school visits and games. The unions have a fear of disturbance in the classroom. They insist on the retention of the leather strap for the punishment of all pupils, boys and girls, from age five upwards. They are reluctant to enter into any discussion on the reduction of belting and refuse to permit even a record of belting to be kept in the schools. That means that nobody in Scotland knows how much belting there is. If a factory foreman hit with a leather strap a child who had committed an offence, there would be an outcry in parliament and the press; but teachers are largely immune from these enquiries. The teachers' unions have become an evasive as the political parties. One reason given by one of the unions against the keeping of records of belting was that the same pupils would feature in it again and again, and that record might fall into the hands of a potential employer. Therefore the keeping of a belting record might spoil a pupil's chances of getting a job when he left school. It's true. They really did say that.

The unions regard the 'recalcitrance' of some pupils as just another of the occupational hazards of teaching, like low salaries and large classes and bad buildings. Therefore when I tried to uphold the pupils who were getting into trouble, it was as if I had defended low salaries and poor buildings. I was regarded as a mine manager who was indifferent to pit damp in a badly ventilated shaft. The militant workers expressed their solidarity against this questioning of their inherent rights.

The analogy of the boss-versus-worker argument was nourished by this emphasis on rights. A teacher had a right to do what he liked in his own classroom. A teacher had a right to use a belt if he wanted to. It was tyrannical to deprive a teacher of any of these human rights. The number of disruptive pupils was increasing slowly. Many of them had disturbed home backgrounds. I talked to parents and pupils and sought to get at the truth of what was biting them. But many teachers felt this was siding with the criminals when we ought to close the ranks against them, and the members of the Education Committee supported them by saying that I was spending too much time with the disruptive pupils. Young teachers, people of goodwill, were confused when pressure was put on them by some older teachers. I want to appeal over the heads of the teachers' unions to the members of the trade unions throughout the country. It is **their** children that the row is about. The trade union movement in Scotland should understand the traditionalist nature of the Scottish teachers' unions. They are attached to the idea of a two-class society. They are part of the establishment's purpose to use the educational system to divide society, and rule. They have allied themselves to an educational system which channels off the docile pupils with promises of honours if they will support the establishment and devote their energies to its services. A headmaster who didn't belt the trouble-making pupils was a cause for concern to the teachers' unions. The members of trade unions outside education should realise that if they are taken in by the appeals for solidarity with the teachers' unions, they are giving these teachers' unions a licence to belt **their** children.

As the number of the malcontent pupils grew, they became individually bolder. Many of them were fortified by the solidarity and support of a gang called the Gringoes; and, perhaps following the example of a first division football club which has a younger group in the reserve league, the gang had a supporting group of 'Young Gringoes'. They had regular meeting places and their propaganda followed the example of political parties, although their public notices were sprayed on available surfaces with aerosol. Like the teachers' unions, too, they put pressure on reluctant members. "The villainy you teach me I will execute, and it shall go hard but I will better the instruction". The leaders of the teachers' unions pointed to the intimidation exercised by the Gringoes. Youngsters ostracised by their gang were in real trouble. Sometimes they were beaten up, at all times isolated and frightened and miserable. Their waking hours were a conflict between the gang whom they feared and their parents whom they respected. There was a bleak inhumanity in gang attitudes. One fifteen year old was beaten up just because he didn't belong to the gang and didn't have gang values; he did his homework and wore the school uniform and had short hair and lived up to his parents' orders and expectations. The gang disliked him. But sometimes there was not even that tenuous reason for a beating-up When another boy was beaten up and we had identified the boys who were responsible and they had admitted it, I asked them what they had against the boy. Had he grassed on them to the police? No. Had he done anything to incur their hatred? No. Why, then, did they dislike him so intensely that they had hit him, knocked him down and kicked his head with heavy boots? They replied that they didn't dislike him, in fact, they hardly knew him. He just happened to be there at the time when there was a fight, a neutral figure, and they set on him.

What should a headmaster do in these circumstances? Usually he makes a public statement denouncing meaningless violence and belts the offenders. Public anger, thirsting for retribution, is assuaged and the incident recedes from the headlines. Because I didn't belt the offenders or make the public denunciation, the incident was kept alive as an example of 'the break-down of law and order'. In Summerhill we were trying to create a school free from the strains that caused this hatred. 'Utopianism' said a critic. In seeking how to heal these wounds that led to violent acts, we got not support from the Scottish Education Department nor the colleges of education nor the universities. They did not feel involved. It was one of the major problems of our civilisation but these agencies weren't giving it active concern. If we did anything other than make the traditional gesture of opposing violence to violence, we laid ourselves open to public attack, and these agencies and the Education Committee washed their hands of us.

Chapter Three

EXTRA-MURAL

A relative of Prime Minister Baldwin who had been a nun wrote a book telling about her escape from the the cloistered life She called it "I Leap Over The Wall". There is the same feeling about the growing development in Scottish schools which is called "extra-mural education". My predecessor had been the north-east's pioneer in informal outdoor education. He'd fought a long campaign to get for the school a cottage in the countryside near the River Dee, twenty miles from the school It is a peaceful place. Sitting outside you can hear the babble of a burn and the wind soughing through the pines. Neighbours come to pass the time of day. Here city children enter into the cosy quietness of rural life. Nearby there is a water-powered sawmill. They cook their own food and the cottage is well situated for day-long journeys into the hills. In the evenings there is time for leisurely talk. I read the account of the preparing of the cottage for occupation by the pupils. Teachers had laboured like galley-slaves digging trenches for plumbing, and repairing the structure. Ten pupils would go there with a teacher for three days at a time.

From spring until autumn some of the staff would take thirty or more pupil's for a day's hike in the mountains. There were hostelling trips farther afield. Groups went to France for their Easter holidays. One school-owned bus was insufficient for the transport demands and the school ran a mammoth fair and bought a second bus. A Manchester trust gave us a third bus when the community club opened and the youth leader took pupils canoeing on the Dee and the Tay and sports teams to play against other schools.

In the evenings the school buzzed like a beehive. There were swimming, indoor football in a lofty games hall, mountaineering training on a specially constructed training wall, canoe-building, table tennis, trampoline, record playing, badminton. The youth wing accommodated in the mornings a nursery play group and the pupils helped to entertain old people on some afternoons. Pupils went out to help old people in their homes, painting and papering a kitchen, or going their errands and just talking to them. There was a vigour about these activities that most of the formal classrooms rarely evoked. The school had bought an old car and the technical staff repaired it and gave the pupils driving lessons in the playground. Go-karts practisedgingerlyround the perimeter. Every year there was a school play, performed with such riotous vigour and obvious enjoyment that the comparison with the tempo of the rest of the school work was significant. It was when the traditonal curriculum was over that the school woke up. The teacher responsible for the school play was also the begetter of the annual magazine. In a national competition it achieved a main award and the judges said it was 'light years ahead' of some of the stodgy productions of well-known traditional schools. The school was like a Festival in which the fringe far outshone the main body.

The Education Committee had been generous to Summerhill. Behind the lavish equipment I could perceive the philosophy of councillors who genuinely wanted to make every provision to persuade the majority of pupils and their parents that they did care about them. That was never in doubt. Somewhere along the line between the councillors who passed the motion and the pupils who were its intended beneficiaries, the communication broke down. It's like a blockage between the people who allocate the money for relief in an earthquake area and the local people who don't get the blankets. This is why I think Summerhill provides a significant study of Scottish life in transition. For example the Education Committee provided a fine hall, seating a thousand, equipped with a cinema projection room and a screen. As far as I could discover, the equipment had not been used. I collected catalogues of films from all over the world and prepared to show them to our pupils, travel films, a magnificent film about Skanderbeg, the national hero of Albania, UNESCO films about life in primitive central American communities, science films, full length feature films like **Culloden,** films from Sweden and Russia and Czechoslovakia and Japan and India, instructional films about botany and the internal combustion engine. It was at this stage that the technical troubles began. There were three 16 mm projectors in the school and none of them could throw a beam from the projection room high above the back of the hall on to the stage. There was much expert consultation but we never got a lens that would meet the requirements. In the meantime we had been showing some of the films from a projector set up in the middle of the hall, but the afternoon sunshine filtering through the breaks in the curtains made the pictures so thin and washy that the pupils lost interest in them. We had to get an adequate blackout. The Education Committee did everything they could to help us, they spent £100 in fitting rails that would make a curtain overlap, but the cords operating the overlaps were so difficult to pull properly that it took a long time to shut out the lignt before the film began. The teachers got tired of the efforts always to be tugging at the cords and gave up the exercise.

In the same way we had to relinquishour dreamsof having a theatre workshop. The stage was richly equipped with flats and lighting, the pupils enjoyed creating their own drama. But an examination-based curriculum didn't admit of the interruptions in formal education that were required if the pupils were to be free over a two or three hour period to settle down into a ploy of this kind. It would all have been much easier to cope with in a small school. And for the same reason we daren't send to the artificial ski-slope for ski training all the pupils who volunteered for it; it would have made too great a hiatus in the examination-orientated classroom lessons. At great expense and against much opposition, the education committee had had the foresight to build an artificial ski-slope, realising that skiing was to become very popular ·in Scotland and realising also the benefits to their teenagers of such an outlet. They had been able to cope with the external opposition to the idea. They were completely unable to cope with the internal opposition from the schools, which was really opposition from the Examination Board. That's a charge the Board would deny, saying that it is possible to pass your examinations and also engage in extra-mural activities. "All this and skiing too". But they cannot deny that it is the pressure of the examinations which makes teachers reluctant to cede time, especially when the pupils are on the borderline between failure and success. There is no integrating authority in Scotland or England to adjudicate between conflicting claims on children's time, examination work or ski training. It is seldom that our unimaginative Scottish schools turn out a Secretary of State who has the understanding and independence to intervene to support a new initiative against the inertia of the machine and the administrators who mind it. I think that this capitulation in face of difficulty, this fear of devising new ways, this unenterprising educational outlook may explain the fear and inertia that holds us back in other spheres, for example in querying the financial restrictions that the 'gnomes of Zurich' impose on us. A people educated to be nimble-minded and enterprising would have addressed a much more thorough-going analysis to that problem. I feel that our politicians and administrators are far too respectful of authority to have the will to stray far from the known ways and blaze new trails. I support a Scottish Assembly, but there is no apparent reason to believe that a Scottish Minister of Education would be any more independent of tradition than a Westminster-based Secretary of State. In fact, Scottish education is less liberal than English education. I have an uneasy feeling that an Edinburgh Assembly would make as little difference to the fundamental Westminster ideas of the nature of government as comprehensive education has made to the work carried out in the classrooms.   It looks like being the same thing, on a smaller scale and for that reason less inert, but nevertheless the same thing. I fear the Edinburgh Minister of Education would be as subservient to the   traditional Educational Institute of Scotland as the Westminister Secretary of State for Scotland is, and as little sympathetic to the second class citizens of our city schools. An Edinburgh governing-elite would not necessarily be more democratic than a London governing-elite, nor more kindly disposed towards our efforts to educate all our pupils to demand participation in government.

It all comes back to this; you can't have an enduring political change unless it is supported by a cultural change; you can't have cultural change until you set the schools free from their present function of being the indoctrinators of the status quo. Change begins in the school,or, as Prime Minister Attlee said, in the minds of men.

The same fate befell Inverlair Lodge.It was a 22-roomed shooting lodge at the back of the Nevis range, a gift that we we were free to accept if we could get the Education Committe to back us. Several years earlier it had been offered to us back in Fife. At that time £1,500 would have set it going, But the Education Committee referred the project to their architects who went to town and produced a plan for a dream castle costing £20,000, which the Education Committee turned down because of the cost. This is the professional obstruction that a reforming social democracy hasn't learned to cope with. It's a glimpse of an advisory system that has got out of hand. At Aberdeen we tried again. Immediately we were faced with all the reasons why we should not proceed with the project. Ten miles out of Aberdeen the Education Committee had a small country house called Tertowie where pupils were sent for a week at a time to go for walks in the peaceful farmlands and study biology or music. The councillors said, "What's wrong with Tertowie?" I replied, "There's nothing wrong with Tertowie. But Inverlair offers something different, experience of living in wild country, of living close to the mountains and of learning about life in a harsh countryside which is part of Scotland's heritage." A Tory dispensation in Aberdeen sent a delegation to see Inverlair and turned the plan down.Then Labour came into power

I wrote memoranda, consulted experts about costs, sanitation, fire precautions, hygiene, grants, curricula, insurance, transport, heating, weather, residential education, water supply, furniture, drying, staffing, decoration. Recently I weighed the files, memoranda and correspondence accumulated over thirteen years. It weighed 28lbs. I took it all into the garden and made a bonfire of it. I made a big conflagration. Dreams were going up in flames. We could have reduced juvenile delinquency in Aberdeen but they wouldn't let us.

An outside committee of people well-known in Scottish national life, had agreed to help to bring the Inverlair dream into reality. They had meetings at Edinburgh and Inverlair and devoted much time to correspondence and consultation, trying to solve the legal and administrative difficulties. These were people on whom the school had no claim. Willingly they had agreed to help because they felt that this was an educational programme which might contribute to Scotland's educational development. They were expert in different fields and their help was valuable. This unselfregarding work of people who felt that the well being of children has a claim upon them, is an encouraging feature of our society. They sought to discover where it was that the scheme had been waylaid and tried to get into motion again. They raised money. They employed a gifted couple to go to Inverlair and bring a deserted building into habitable conditions. The husband was a civil engineer and handyman who had been also a theatre producer. His wife was an actress. They both responded to the charm of Inverlair and established good relations with ther neighbours and entered into the ceilidhs of Lochaber and laboured to create a centre where Aberdeen children could enjoy these things. We sent two pupils at a time to help. During the day they laboured and in the evenings they listened to stories or readings. I asked two of them how they had enjoyed their fortnight at Inverlair. They said, "It was good. We had to work hard. We discovered that the woman was an actress, and an artist. But she was all right. In the evenings they read stories to us".

"What stories?"

"Lots of poems by Burns, and other stories. There were stories about strange beasts. We liked them especially."

"Which book did these stories about beasts come from?"

"I think they said it was the book of Ezekiel.'

I hadn't thought of Ezekiel as a book of bedtime stories.

The old building mellowed under their attention.The bedrooms were decorated in finely chosen,contrasting colours. Two ground floor rooms were knocked into one to make a diningroom. A brick fireplace was removed and an old farm-kitchen swey was revealed for holding pots over a peat fire. The floor was of large flagstones. The whole room was a grey monochrome. Then I went in one day and found they had completed their redecoration. They had put up brilliant scarlet curtains. It was a staggering,and beautiful, effect. I visualised the effect on the pupils.Drifting with dully, unseeing eyes through their environment they would be brought up against the discriminating use of colour. It's the spirit of Stevenson's prayer, 'Stab my spirit broad awake."

That was part of the intention of Inverlair. Near the house there was a millwheel on which was an inscription which said it belonged to Angus the Miller and the date was the fourteenth century. Just outside the commonroom window was a knoll topped by a cairn which commemorated the burial of seven headless bodies killed in a clan feud. The heads had been carried to the clan chief at Invergarry, being washed at a well beside Loch Garry which is now known as the Well of the Seven Heads. Much more ancient, on the mountains opposite the house are horizontal lines like roads marking the levels washed by the waters of ancient lochs before the ice ages. We had all sorts of plans ready to put into effect. On a hill pedestal we were going to site a telescope to make moon observations because the rain-softened highland air is so clear of dust. From this centre our Aberdeen recalcitrants would explore the West Highlands from Argyll to Sutherland, sleeping in a line of bothies we had engaged so that they should not be burdened on their journey with tents. There would be peat-cutting and tree-felling and pony trekking and sailing and mountaineering. And a studio where, in the evenings, they would paint and write and carve deerhorn. And a library, and a library fire beside which, on a winter evening, they could stretch out and, untroubled by television, read the stories of the old storytellers. "With a tale he cometh to you, with a tale that keepeth children from play and old men from the chimney corner."

All unfulfilled dreams. We still believe we held the secret of one way to bring up our children to be happy and responsible and self-fulfilling. When evening came they would be tired out with the effort of a day's climbing or gardening or tree-sawing or cooking or house decorating. The actress who put up the curtains was going to tell them how to collect thistledown to fill cushions and pillows. Old recipes, old stories, old beliefs, magic, would be part of their cultural background. Once during a break, eating our sandwiches and drinking our coffee on the knoll beside the lodge, we listened while she told us a story of witches who were dancing widdershins round a bonfire.

"Widdershins?" I asked

"It means, the wrong way," she explained. "Opposite to the direction the sun takes round the earth. That's the way the witches always danced."

Our pupils would have been fascinated by that part of our Scottish tradition. There was much in Inverlair that would have caught their imagination.

But Inverlair wasn't to be only a culture of exploring corries and listening to old tales while the flames burned in the fireside and threw flickering shadows on the walls. We wanted to implicate our pupils in the story of Scotland's present and its future, the making of aluminium and paper, the bringing of life back to the glens. And for that purpose the Summerhill curriculum would be adapted to prepare pupils, before they set out for Inverlair, to understand what the exhibits at Carrbridge and Kingussie and Newtonmore had to offer them and wander through the region with a seeing eye.

Our programme was to send 30 pupils to Inverlair for a month at a

time. We estimated that all the pupils in the school would be offered
the opportunity to spend a month there during their school career. We
would try and integrate the Inverlair activities with classroom work
in Summerhill. It wasn't to be just a month out of their studies when
they would have a programme of greater physical activity. This is
what separated Inverlair from the outdoors projects of other Scottish
schools. Most of them see an extra-mural centre as providing a
health-giving change of activity which will send pupils back to their
classrooms refreshed and readier to accept the dour slog of
traditional study. We were trying to devise a new curriculum free
from the memorising of irrelevant detail and from the division into
subject compartments. We were trying to provide a new answer to the
question: how do you educate Scottish teenagers? We would show
them in concrete, manageable terms, the aftermath of Culloden and
also the restorative work of Telford, crofting tenure, tourist
possibilities, soil analysis and soil reclamation. This would be the
main part of the work. Textbooks and classroom studies would be
contributory, explaining to pupils the problems as they arose.
Geology, nature study, history, mathematics would not be separate
things, but treasure houses to be ransacked for clues to illuminate the
mysteries that presented themselves in their journeys or
food-growing or archaeological digs (for example discovering the
difference between the crosssections of a Wade and a Telford road).
Culture would not be a veneer, the acceptable and superficial
knowledge of what we'd been brought up to regard as "educated men
and women" but the essential food of living. We'd gone back to first
and last things and asked, in a crisis in the history not only of Scotland
but of western civilisation, how do we bring up Scottish children to
live fully and happily in an integrated society of which they all feel
they are full members? We felt we would at last really get to grips
with education and were prepared to follow where our discoveries
led, which might be towards de-schooling, we didn't know.

Earlier I had written to the Scottish Education Department
outlining what we had in mind and saying we had heard they
controlled funds for educational research and would they let us have
some money. They replied that while they commended the work we
were doing, it could not be regarded as educational research, being
more properly described as curricular development and therefore
was not eligible for a grant. I asked a lecturer in the School of
Education in Nottingham University why he thought the Scottish
Education Department didn't regard our venture as coming under
the description of educational research and he replied: "Because you
didn't have statistics."

We got letters from teachers, and also from parents, all over the
world (they still keep arriving), asking if they could come and work at
Inverlair or send their children full time. English educationists

offered support and so did the staff of the Education Department of the University of Stirling. But the more extreme of the traditionalists in the Summerhill staff were unenthusiastic and so were the Director of Education and his committee. They disapproved of us probably in the same way as the Mother Superior disapproved of Monica Baldwin who leapt over the wall.

Chapter Four

THE NEW COMPREHENSIVE

And then the school became comprehensive. "All-through comprehensive" was the description. It meant that the pupils arrived at the age of 12 and could remain until they were 18. What difference did comprehensive education make?

The builders had completed a big, new, four-storey building housing the homecraft, physics, chemistry, biology and geography departments, and the library. There was a games hall, a youth centre, a new bungalow for the art department, an extension of the technical department and new dining halls. The Education Committee had been generous in their provision. They had done everything they could to ensure that the children of working class parents in a new housing estate in Aberdeen should have classrooms and equipment as good as any school in the land. Parents visiting the science departments were astounded by the wealth of scientific equipment. The lofty games hall measured up to international standards for badminton, it had a climbing wall where pupils could practise mountaineering in a less chilling atmosphere, it had nets separating groups playing different games. In the youth centre pupils could get a hair-do in the hairdressing section, prepare coffee in a formidable-looking coffee machine, dance, listen to records or build a canoe. The medical section had an expensive-looking dentist's chair. An expensive language lab was being installed. There were tape recorders, a video-tape recorder, television sets, photocopiers, overhead projection equipment, telephone linkage between departments, a clinic where a full-time nurse was in attendance, rest rooms, a speech therapy room. Skilled advice was readily available on buildings, equipment, in-service courses, health, physical education, audio-visual aids, science, technical education, remedial education, careers, psychology.

When a civilisation is on the skids, it is very difficult for the student to diagnose the trouble from a study of generalisations and massive abstractions. The human mind finds itself more at home with homely details, manageable experience. Maybe if I talk about one school and its daily experience in the midst of a period of transition in national and world history, I'll be able to make clearer what were the issues which affected men's thinking and children's lives.

The first hint of trouble came when Aberdeen Education Committee were considering what name to give. to their new comprehensive schools. The term "comprehensive" is unattractive, unimaginative, heavy, perhaps incomprehensible. I wrote to the local newspaper suggesting that we should avoid these prestigious, boastful terms — Academy, College, High School — and just say simply "Summerhill School".

I did try to put myself in the shoes of these Labour members of the committee. They were pledged to an educational revolution, and enthusiastic about it. The campaign was over, the battle had been won; it was a time for the entering into a major reform, a righting of wrongs and injustice. There was a new world beginning. Success induces a feeling of generosity. They could afford to sit back and consider carefully the first steps.

The new ideas of comprehensive education were counter-weighing the traditional ideas. The balance was swinging and might have come down on either side. The Labour Education Committee were divided about the choice of name. I think that maybe for the first time some of them began to think in terms of the work that would go on in a new comprehensive school; the framework would be different, and would the work in the individual classroom also be different? Or was the ancient Scottish system of education a pearl of great price which must not be lost? Some of the committee were swayed by the advice of an external member, the retired head of the University's Department of Education. He was a kind, respected figure. These members were also part of the tradition which is respectful (I think unnecessarily respectful) towards university figures. He said "Academy", and "Academy" it was for all of Aberdeen's comprehensive schools. It was as simple and honest as that.

What's in a name? There may be much in a name. We were engaged in a battle which for the present was about two names. Labour had won the first battle; the new state system was to be called "comprehensive". The establishment accepted their defeat there, and like the wily old campaigners they are, they set about ensuring that it was only the name that would be changed. The generic name of the schools would be changed to "comprehensive" but the reality (the classroom work) would remain unchanged. They were giving up the shadow, and battling to retain the substance.

In those critical days, Aberdeen's decision to call their schools **academies** tipped the balance. The traditionalists hadn't wholly lost even the battle of names. We conform to the name stuck on us. These academies would retain the Scottish academic tradition.

One of the elite schools of the old dispensation was called Aberdeen Academy. So what were Aberdeen parents to assume about the new situation in which all Aberdeen's comprehensive schools were to be called academies? Obviously that the comprehensives were to model themselves on Aberdeen Academy. And this is what has happened. Aberdeen's comprehensive schools are not different in outlook and policy from Aberdeen Academy and Aberdeen Grammar School. No sooner was the battle for comprehensive education won than it was lost.

That is another reason for saying that no political revolution can succeed unless it is under-pinned by an educational revolution. The Labour members of Aberdeen Education Committee failed to defend the comprehensive revolution because their ideas on education came from their own upbringing in establishment-controlled schools. They could think independently about politics. They had no background on which to think independently about education. Their ideas on education had already long been manipulated. They were puppets dancing to the educational strings of their schooling.

That's what this book is about. How do we go about the defence of political gains? How do we use our experience in order to plan our next advance on the citadels of educational privilege? Basically Aberdeen Labour councillors' failure to bring a new comprehensive system into operation was due to their failure to think in any terms but those of the past. It was a failure of initiative, of imagination. I recalled T. E. Lawrence's comments on the treaty-makers at Versailles when for a brief moment there was the possibility that a new world might be born. "We stammered that we were building a new heaven and a new earth, but the old men thanked us kindly and made their peace." The Versailles rebirth, like the Comprehensive rebirth, was a still birth. The establishment had been careful to ensure that, as children, these councillors had had no practice or experience or confidence in devising alternative schemes of government or education. It was not the purpose of their education to suggest alternative schemes which might put the old academies out of business.

I shuddered at the name and feared its influence. The Labour councillors in choosing the name "academy" were reinforcing the Scottish tradition which made frequent use of the word "academic". It was not merely a bad omen. You can defy an omen. It revealed the failure of the Aberdeen Council to understand what comprehensive education is about and to appreciate the nature of the promise it contained. The same old examinations, the same old wielding of the belt, the same authoritarian attitudes, the same neglect of the majority of working class children; these were the things forecast by this choice of name. And that was how it turned out. Today all the Aberdeen ''comprehensives'' are essentially the same as the traditional Scottish secondary schools that they were designed to replace.

But none of this troubled the comprehensive euphoria of the speeches of the opening day.

The school newspaper in an open letter to the then ex-Secretary of State, Mr William Ross, said: "In welcoming you to open this comprehensive school, we acknowledge the vision that blueprinted a new kind of school and the generosity of the local authority who made it a reality. But this is only the beginning of the story. We have a long, long way to go before Aberdeen parents outgrow the old selective senior secondary idea that ability is given only to a few. We have discovered that throughout the school population there is a wealth of ability hitherto unrecognised. It will be our job to nourish this ability and bring it to fruit.

"A new approach is necessary (and that implies a reduction in corporal punishment). We see comprehensive education as an equal concern for all."

Opening the school, Mr Ross said: "I believe starting here in this part of Aberdeen may well be something that will be a pointer to the possibilities and potential of education in Scotland and something that we can look back on not just in Aberdeen but throughout Scotland as bringing into reality part of the vision that was behind the concept of our comprehensive education. . . .

"We forgot for years and years the great mass of the population whose potential never was realised and I am glad to say that report after report and commission after commission have drawn our attention to the fact of the unrealised potential of the great bulk of the boys and girls of this country. We are only now starting along the road of the realisation of that potential and in this development of Scottish tradition it doesn't end just with the creating of what is called a comprehensive school, it is the work that will go on within that comprehensive school, it is the way that headmasters and teachers approach the idea of organising towards the comprehensive school that will determine whether or not it is successful."

He spoke of his support of the junior secondary school. Its great defect, he said, was that it was selective. "But its great advantage that was never properly realised in Scottish education was that there was no external examination in the Junior Secondary School, and that meant there was no pressure upon the curriculum, it wasn't moulded from above by a university or by external examination from the demands of a university. If there was any defect in Scottish education probably over many years it was the lack of experment; probably less experiment in Scottish education than there was in English education. . . ."

He felt that the comprehensive school would enrich the country at a time when we needed every man, every woman coming from our schools to be conscious of their own abilities and of their own responsibilities. He wanted us to help create a more satisfying, cohesive community. "There are no people more idealistic than young people but that idealism is often starved by older people set in their ways and turning their backs on what the youngsters are demanding and what they are groping at. That's what I want to see turned out from the schools, youngsters who will question, youngsters who will be critical and while questioning the old ideas will equally question the new ideas, because there are many of the new ideas that are of even less value than the old. To the extent to which there is a jumping on the band wagons of new ideas that are destructive of community life, to that extent too there is a gap in educational achievement in the fulfilment of our personalities. I regard this school as a new school and a new departure in education and I hope that teachers, education authority, headmaster and pupils all appreciate that the future of this kind of school probably depends on each and every one of you, your response to leadership and your participation of leadership."

He said there was an embarrassment for him in opening Summerhill Academy. He referred to the book I had written about Braehead School in Fife, **The Sins of the Children.** "I opened the book in the House of Commons because I always like to prepare myself for everything I'm going to do; you get plenty of time, it's a nice quiet place, the House of Commons. Then I saw on the cover of this book, 'As we go to press, the Secretary of State for Scotland has confirmed the proposal of Fife County Council to close the school'. Who do you think the Secretary of State was? Him" (pointing to himself). Then turning to me he said, "I believe you took great pride and pleasure in what you did at Braehead, but there is an even greater challenge here and it's a challenge in respect of which I am perfectly sure you will gather round you teachers dedicated to education. I hope you will get the co-operation that you must get, the co-operation of the parents who will appreciate that what we are trying to do is educate for the whole child and for all children, and with that and the response of the children themselves we will start to create a fine, new and worthy tradition of Scottish education. Summerhill Academy. Summerhill, you know, is a name that is renowned and if you mention it in any educational circles, they all know Summerhill. Nothing to do with Aberdeen, nothing at all; it's to do with a man called A. S. Neill. He wasn't an Aberdonian, he was born at Forfar and educated at Edinburgh. But he is a man who spent his whole life experimenting in education, a man who made mistakes and admits he made mistakes, but a man who gained something of value and brought new values to old ideas of education, and I think he has done much. His name is known throughout the world; Summerhill is the name of his school. Now we have a new Summerhill, a Summerhill Academy that has been part of the educational system of Scotland. I hope that it may well be that this Summerhill, Summerhill Academy, will be as well known in the future for the pioneering work, for the successful work of furthering worthy ideas within Scottish education. And I wish you my very, very best wishes for the success of Summerhill Academy. And let me say a word to the boys and girls. It all depends on you. You are all part of it, you are not just pupils of the school, you are part of the school and in a sense you are the first, and you are going to throw out your chest in the future and you are going to proclaim to the whole of Aberdeen and Scotland, 'We were at Summerhill Academy'. It's you who are going to create that tradition by your co-operation with your teachers, by your groping towards the truth and by your ability to be worthy citizens of a very, very fine and worthy city. Lord Provost, I am very proud indeed to be asked officially to open Summerhill Academy, and I do so in all humility, knowing full well that with the efforts of all, it will be a proud day and seen to be a proud day in the annals of Aberdeen education.''

I had greeted the selection of Mr Ross to open the school without enthusiasm, since he had agreed to the closing down of Braehead in Fife. But as I sat on the platform on the opening day and listened to his speech, I responded to the genuine warmth of his attitude. He really was on our side. He had the grace to admit to embarrassment in opening Summerhill. There are limitations (I told myself) to what even a Secretary of State can do in a local situation. The things he had been saying about education were the things I believed in. The Labour gospel had been restated and the Labour Party's vision of the comprehensive school was clearly and brightly outlined, as a picture on the television screen is brought back into focus. True, the convener of Aberdeen Education Committee, feeling perhaps that Mr Ross had gone overboard in his concern for the majority of ordinary pupils, restated the tradition and said that we would still have to put academic education high on our list of priorities. But I felt between the Secretary of State's reassertion of the first principles of comprehensive education and the Education Convener's gloss on that statement, the Secretary of State would more reliably represent the official intention and I thawed in this more promising climate. I walked with Mr Ross through the school and I got the impression that this was not a Secretary of State performing a chore but a teacher who had a genuine concern for children and in the launching of a new experiment in education to help them. He lingered in classrooms, chatting to pupils, resisting the promptings of aides who reminded him of another appointment. He further upset his timetable to intervene, on invitation, in a senior pupils' debate. They nailed him with questions and supplementary questions, asked with independence and courtesy, and he replied in the same manner. This was the kind of communication I had long envisaged, tomorrow's voters, young people from a working-class housing estate, with ease and confidence interrogating the Secretary of State, and he with grace and good humour seeking to answer their questions. It was a dialogue between equals from which as a spectator I drew hope. This was different from my feudal upbringing and schooling. This wasn't the laird with grace and superiority presenting the prizes to the children of his tenants; nor a tribune of the people who had "risen" until he was able to take over the laird's function. This was for real. There was a new world beginning.

But, as our later experience at Summerhill showed, there wasn't a new world beginning. I believe that future historians will try and discover why the Labour vision became more and more blurred in the seventies and the high hopes faded. In the Summerhill story they will find a particular example of what happened. I am sure Mr Ross did mean what he said about ending the tyranny of the examinations and developing "the unrealised potential of the great bulk of the boys and girls of this country". He understood, as other Ministers didn't, that the setting up of a comprehensive school was only the beginning of the battle. I think he is an honest man, not able to be bought by the flattery of high society or the bribes of industry. He speaks with an unashamed Scottish accent, his vowels, like his principles, unmodified by the Westminster and English-public-school influence. But he underestimated the forces glowering at this comprehensive experiment, determined on its destruction and, when the going got difficult at Summerhill, he refrained from intervention.

Parents wandering through the school on the opening day were astonished at the wealth of provision in the games hall, the sophisticated scientific and technical equipment, the gaiety of paintings and pottery and wood carvings in the art rooms. Several of them said, "We were born too early. School wasn't like this in our day." But at the back of their minds there was a doubt. These doubts in people's minds are the background to any transition period in history; you don't really understand the period unless you understand clearly the crowded, colliding ideas in people's minds, some of them rarely articulated. The parents of Aberdeen don't think highly of art. Some Act of Parliament somewhere had laid it down that you had to have art but they didn't know why. They were prepared to receive it respectfully; no doubt the educationists knew what they were doing; and it provided an outlet for pupils who were good at art — they could become art teachers or get a well-paid job in commercial art. But that was off the main line of education. Life is real, life is earnest, and unless you are "going in for art", art won't get you anywhere. Nevertheless they observed that their children were enjoying splashing paint on paper, giving expression to their imaginings, and they were glad to see their children enjoying themselves. But they were not convinced; they made their unspoken reservations. And drama was the same. To produce a play was playing, and life in the north-east of Scotland is too important a business for playing. They didn't condemn theatre shows as their grandfathers did. Their grandfathers referred to them angrily as "play-acting" (a double condemnation). The new generation of parents were more tolerant; nevertheless they had residual doubts. Their attitude on what subjects in school are really important was indicated by a letter I had from a parent. We had been discussing religious freedom and some pupils asked why they had to have lessons in religious education. I said that on the form which their parents had filled up when the pupils first came to Summerhill, there was a question asking whether they wanted their children to take part in religious education or not, and that all parents had, in fact, said they wanted their children to take part in religious education. I added that if some of them had changed their minds and would send me a note saying so, I would see that these children did not have to attend these lessons.

I got half a dozen letters. One of them said that Christina's arithmetic was needing attention and the parents thought that her time would be better spent in more lessons in arithmetic than in religious education. And there spoke, I believe, the authentic north-east voice. Religion, like art and drama, doesn't help you to get a job and a good wage.

It's only in the last two decades that religion has so lost ground in Aberdeen as to be equated with art and drama. A generation ago a materialistic presbyterianism was a necessary part of a child's upbringing. A kirk connection helped you to get a job.

The Summerhill story is tied up with this recession in religion. Lytton Strachey said that Dr Arnold of Rugby expected his pupils to help the "good poor". I know exactly what he meant by that. The good poor were identified by their respect for their social betters, their docility and their church connection. They grew into the ambitious poor. In the Summerhill area were many working-class parents who were ambitious for their children, eager that they should toe the line at school, wear the school blazer, become prefects and pass the examinations in order that, as a reward for these observances, they might get a good job. But, as the church congregations diminished, one powerful voice exhorting the poor to be good, diminished. The sergeant-major voice of the kirk, rallying the ranks, became a whisper. Some of the good poor fell out; the ranks were depleted. Bunyan's Apollyon said that there is no king who will lightly lose his subjects, and the twentieth-century Apollyon is an equally resilient character. He reinforced the Scottish Certificate of Education Examination Board and promoted it to take over the function previously exercised by the Church. Before then, you were unlikely to get a good job unless you had a Church connection; now you were unlikely to get a good job unless you had an Examination Board connection. The Examination Board has as little to do with education as the church had to do with religion. Their function is to exercise discipline, to keep the poor good — that is, toeing the line, respectful, saying the right things. And the replacement for the Church, the Examination Board, was successful. The voice of the Examination Board, bawling across the parade ground of the school, reasserted the authority the Church had lost and marshalled the reluctant pupils back into the ranks. Although I support neither the old Ecclesiastical Board (the Church) nor the new Examination Board, I can scarcely forbear to cheer the Establishment on its survival. Audacity is always admirable. The new board's success more than compensated for the old board's failure. There was a gain in establishment recruits.

Nevertheless a growling danger like distant thunder menaced the victory. Drunk with victory, the Establishment was overreaching itself. As the Church's voice diminished and even a nominal adherence to values other than material values evaporated, the more blatantly materialistic did the Establishment become. The materialism was powerfully reinforced by the advertising of unadulterated materialism on television, commercial and B.B.C. In the Summerhill area, that meant that more and more women went out to work; and that meant that parents had less and less time and patience to give to their children. The parents counted for less and less. The kids were on their own. Now, unconsciously, parents transmit the values of the past. Therefore, when there was less communication with children, there was less transmission of these values. Obviously the Establishment hadn't thought about that. Compelled to make their own meals, fill their own evenings and weekends, the children learned self-reliance. They became independent earlier. They began to think their own thoughts and, like all individuals who feel menaced, to club together into like groups. These groups have now unconsciously coalesced and in our authoritarian society have become the only effective opposition to the Scottish Certificate of Education Examination Board.

Their influence grows, perhaps in the same way as the African Zimbabwe or Frelimo groups' influence grew, a gathering together for mutual protection. As they become aware of their strength they begin to find a wild, fearful pleasure in the exercise of power. They put pressure on the "good" children not to conform. They intimidate them. The pressures are, not to wear the uniform, not to do the homework, not to co-operate with the teachers, to wear jeans and have long hair. Some of the pupils who come from "good" homes ally themselves naturally with their peer group and are accepted. Others, loyal to their parents or frightened of their parents' disapproval, stay outwith the peer group and are penalised, sometimes viciously and violently. Others are confused, torn between two loyalties. Usually

these pupils refuse to give inform tion to teachers or police when
questioned about fights, break-ins, stealing, destruction. Sometimes
the refusal was due to loyalty, sometimes to fear of victimisation.
Occasionally parents came to see me about children terrorised by
their classmates, not sleeping at night, fearing to go to school next
day, life one long, unremitting misery month after month. Some of
them expected me to belt the terrorisers into submission and produce
a reign of security under the law. Most of these parents understood
when I explained that such action would only make life harder for
their son (or, occasionally, daughter). I pointed out that the boy had to
live with his schoolmates and their hostility could make life hell for
him; even if they never laid a hand on him, they could still make life
hell. The gang had understood the sophistications of suffering they
could impose by ostracism and the withdrawing of the ordinary
communications and fellowship. Rarely, a parent would go on
demanding punishment for the gang who were terrorising his son,
even when I asked the parent if it was his own hurt feelings that he
wanted retribution for. I usually found support when I explained what
I would try to do. I would try to gain for the boy reconciliation with his
group. Frequently this was possible. I met about four of the gang
responsible for the ostracism. The conversation followed a pattern
something like this.

"Why do you dislike Jack?"

"We don't dislike Jack."

"Have you got something against him?"

"No."

"You know that he's having a tough time."

(No answer.)

"Do you feel he's against you? Has he clyped (a Scottish word
meaning told tales) to a teacher or something like that?"

"No."

The "noes" were genuine enough. We were in a desolate no-man's
land. I was under suspicion as an agent of the enemy. They weren't
hostile, only coldly indifferent, doubtful. Looking back now I can
sense the conflict going on within them, the hatred of the school on one
hand and the unwillingness to inflict pain on the other. I appeared as a
suppliant. I said, "I can't help Jack. You know that. I could belt the
daylights out of you if I wanted to and I don't want to and it wouldn't
help Jack. Only you can help him. He's going through hell. And as far
as I can make out, the only reason is that his folks are — well, middle
class. Will you give him a break?"

There would be an uncomfortable silence and then usually one of
them would volunteer sturdily, "Aye, we'll do that." I said thank you
and away they went.

A few days later I'd meet Jack and ask him how he was getting on.
"All right now," he'd say cheerfully.

But it didn't always work out like that. There was no possibility of reconciliation for some of the boys who had been proscribed by their group. I know how pupils felt at these encounters. I've felt the same myself when trying to make up my mind whether I was being needlessly cruel (or even vicious) in rejecting an appeal, or a sap in agreeing to it. When pupils felt that the adult world was irredeemably hostile, when they had been belted by their teachers and parents (which I knew to be true), they identified me with the adult world of parents, teachers, police and police court officials, and they terrorised a classmate because he had allied himself with that world. He had accepted the advantages of collaboration with that benefit-conferring world. Teachers (with that obtuseness which some traditionalist teachers continue to display) had praised him in class while contrasting his ready compliance with the surly obstruction of the other pupils. The boy was pleasant, not a tale-bearer, nor a fighter. The civilisation into which he had been born forced him into an impossible situation. I don't know what thoughts went through the heads of these boys who were the victims of brutal assaults by their fellows; but I can guess. They must have shivered with fear at the fulsome praise of some of the teachers, knowing what its repercussions would be. Their own friends would disengage from the conflict and, like most adults in a similar situation, sit on the fence.

This was one of the charges against Summerhill, that we permitted gangsterism and took no action against gang members who beat up pupils not in their gangs. The Labour councillors said there was a softness in us that prevented us taking appropriate retribution; we were too soft with the thugs, and honest, well-doing pupils suffered. The implication is that if we had belted the gangsters there would have been sweetness and light throughout the school. I don't blame the councillors for taking this over-simple view of our society. Other agencies promulgate this doctrine. The B.B.C. consistently supports it. Julian Pettifer in a **Panorama** programme about the increase of juvenile delinquency, harped on this theme that social workers and the people who wanted to change approved schools are a lily-livered lot, and that all right-minded citizens would support the police in their demand for harsher penalties. In the B.B.C.'s **Nationwide** programme, Michael Barratt, ex-Rector of the University of Aberdeen, never misses an opportunity to ally himself with the views of the officers' mess.

It's a dangerous doctrine because it means writing off a growing number of pupils, disinheriting them, outlawing them. All societies have sought to establish peace or at any rate the semblance of peace, by suppressing those dissident elements that they couldn't assimilate. A revolution is usually a victory for the libertarians, but the suppressors gradually move in and undo some of its work. It is hardly surprising that the suppressors are the upper and middle classes who have the tools of suppression and the agencies of thought-control in their power. Each generation tries to widen the area of.conciliation, seeking to permit and even support some of the dissidence; and then it clamps down on the rest. Our generation has made some contribution to enlarging the area of permitted dissidence; and, like its predecessors, it is using its tools and agencies (army, law, church, police, B.B.C., schools, main newspapers and political parties) to clamp down elsewhere. In Summerhill one of the agencies most opposed to the work we were doing was the Church. Various denominations — Church of Scotland, Episcopalians, Catholics and Baptists — achieved an unusual unity in denouncing the school. The core of the debate was that we were trying to conciliate an area of dissidence that the politicians had decided to suppress.

Politicians said that we were spending too much time on the dissident minority and that as a result the majority were suffering. One of Christ's most revolutionary ideas was contained in his parable of the ninety-and-nine sheep whom the shepherd left on the hillside so that he could go and look for the sheep which was lost. It was typical of the churches that they didn't like this parable. Like them I used to think it was nonsense; the well-being of the majority should take precedence over the care of a troublesome minority. Now I'm not so sure. I think that perhaps Christ got it right and that even on purely economic grounds it would pay us to follow his advice. It's a frighteningly revolutionary doctrine but maybe at this crisis of civilisation it's the only doctrine that will work. It says that we do not close our doors as long as there is even one member of the human family outside, unreconciled. It means that in devising a better society we have to use an imaginative power and an ingenuity hitherto reserved to science and technology. It means jettisoning the old doctrine of the expendable minority.

When the politicians talk of a recalcitrant minority, it's not difficult for them to drum up support for repressive measures. But it's different when they talk of individuals. Once in Hitler's Germany a family told me how much they hated the Jews, but when I asked if they knew any Jews, they readily admitted that they had neighbours who were Jews and they were very kind people. "But," they hastened to add, "they were not typical." One might almost say that our civilisation is decaying because we have got used to talking in generalisations instead of talking in terms of individual people.

It was the individual pupils I had in mind when these storms raged at staff meetings and town council meetings. There was Charlie, who told a teacher that he'd stick a knife in him. That sounded bad. It was the incident that triggered off the succession of events that led to my suspension. Much later a teacher in whom Charlie confided, told me the background. Charlie's mother was in hospital and he was worried about her and he was living at home alone. His cat was ill. He sat up all

night with it but the cat died. Then he went to school. He had a quarrel
with one of his pals. Then a teacher spoke sharply to him for
inattention. Charlie replied sharply. The teacher spoke angrily back.
Then Charlie said that he'd stick a knife in him. To the public it may
have sounded like a declaration of war, but it was only the anguished
cry of a desperate youngster.

There were many such incidents. There was a family from a home
that had broken up. They were sent away to a series of substitute
homes — foster parents, residential care, assessment centre, remand
home, approved school, borstal, prison. From some of these places
they would break out and just hang around the area of their own home
and the school until they were picked up and sent away again. They
were looking for something. Latterly one of them would appear at the
school during breaks and organise beatings-up and window breaking.
I went out and brought him back to my room and we had a long talk
and he said he would keep away from the area of the school. But
shortly afterwards he was back, ringleading trouble. When I went to
search for him he dodged round the school. Once I doubled back and
met him alone. I said he'd promised to keep away from the school and
he'd broken his promise. "Lots of people have broken their promises
to me," he said sullenly.

Some had grievous wounds and would have needed a long time of
shelter and healing. One or two needed skilled psychiatric attention.
But the majority of pupils who caused trouble in the classroom were
neither wounded nor disturbed. They needed neither a sanctuary nor
a psychiatrist, only some ordinary care and affection and humour
and support. That such care is not forthcoming is puzzling and
disturbing. Most societies have had a blind area (whether to burning
witches or employing tiny children in coal mines, or using a strap or
cane against children who are inattentive in school) which is
inexplicable to later generations. There is no insoluble problem of
juvenile delinquency. It is just that our society has no wish to help
these pupils. Its mentality is rigid, static; it wants to hang on to its
gods of status and examination certificates and punishment at
whatever cost.

The Summerhill story is the story of what happens to a group of
teachers who try to help these pupils. The school had been fortunate in
some of the teachers I had managed to recruit. I am sad to have to
admit that the majority of the best teachers we recruited came from
outwith Scotland. Two young teachers, a married couple, came to us
from their teacher training at the School of Education in Bristol. The
husband was a graduate of Canberra, his wife a graduate of Oxford.
With the idealism and vigour of youth they applied themselves to this
question of how to educate the majority of the population in a time of
transition and changing values. They were warmhearted and
imaginative in their attitude to their pupils but coldly analytical and

objective in their attitude to their own results. It seemed to me that they represented a new generation of teachers who combined artistic and creative ability with cold scientific realism. Maybe the best research workers in science have always been like that. With detachment they examined the received views, the class antagonisms of Aberdeen, the residual Calvinist attitudes, the faith in "intelligence quotients", the middle-class values. The 12- and 13-year-olds whom they taught were the new barbarians, who in a new Aberdeen situation (in which the influence of the Church had decayed, boys' brigade and scouts were decaying, parents were busy working overtime) had escaped the contagion of the values previously communicated by Church, scouts and parents. They were independent, undoctrinated. And these working class pupils met two middle-class teachers who had escaped from their own indoctrination, and there they all were in a state of liberation, together (teachers and pupils), investigating the present and the future. It was a heart-warming situation, and occasionally a heartbreak.

The teachers had the honesty to tell me about their failures; they came bleakly describing it. Long ago I read **Arrowsmith**, Sinclair Lewis's tale of a medical research worker. Recently I re-read it and was fortified in this story of continued endeavour and failure and partial success and enduring hope.

The two young teachers were investigating not bacteriology like Arrowsmith but education, and with similar results. The only difference was that bacteriology had a tradition of research; there was a climate of opinion favourable to free enquiry into bacteriology. But education was still the subject of almost religious belief, and to initiate an enquiry implied a defiance of the educational authorities who were responsible for imposing these beliefs. This was the forbidding situation in which these young teachers found themselves and against which they battled with fortitude. Research is always a difficult activity but particularly at a time when the area of research is changing from being an area of priestly belief into one of scientific enquiry.

These teachers came to me with pupil magazines so well written that they justified their wildest expectations; and then with stories of the bitterness and hatred and alienation expressed by pupils, which seemed to justify the people who believed in original sin. They were up against it; they were working on the frontiers of education. And, like Arrowsmith, against all the discouragement they carried on.

There was a year-master, a Cambridge graduate whose Cambridge accent in no way prevented him from communicating with these children of Aberdeen trawl fishermen and mill workers. Children are gloriously unaware of bars — colour bars, class bars, accent bars, intelligence quotient bars — unless the discrimination is forced upon them. He would say, "I'm sorry I lost my temper with you this morning. I wasn't feeling too good. There were a few things that upset me." And with childlike magnanimity they forgave him. This is one of the things that the rigid Scottish hierarchy doesn't begin to understand, the capacity for forgiveness that exists under the most sullen, forbidding exterior. He was a new phenomenon on the formal Scottish scene, a fallible adult. Scottish teachers, like the Pope, present the image of infallibility, a remote perfection in which the pupils feel they have no part. And then along comes somebody who seems to be as fallible, sinful, forgiving as they are themselves and they feel relieved, and relax.

Over and above this uncommon admission of common humanity he had an unusual skill in teaching. We invited the parents to spend evenings in the school as learners, so that they could realise what a lesson in art, science, physical education, technical education or English was like. I joined the parents at a desk while he took the lesson. He showed a piece of film about an invasion of a myriad flock of birds on a house and then he discussed it with the parents. The discussion, and especially the recall of detail, enriched the experience. One of them had noticed that the fingernails of the woman in the film were just like the birds' claws. There was good humour in the discussion and a mounting interest as more and more parents became involved. Not only did the parents understand better the nature of English teaching in the school and the part their children played in it; the parents enjoyed the lesson.

It was this teacher who suggested that two senior boys, who had been making much trouble in the school, should spend the whole of their last term helping in a mental hospital for old men. I made the stipulation that they should come and see me every Friday morning to report on what they had done in the hospital during the week. I enjoyed listening to them. They became articulate, and I think they may have gained from the experience of recalling and discussing the events of the week. The hospital staff said that they didn't expect them to take part in all the unpleasant duties of the ward but the boys insisted in doing their full share, cleaning soiled sheets and clearing up a mess. Previously, in school they had been suspicious and sullen, but now there was a geniality about them. They recounted the details of their work with a humorous realism. One of them told me about a concert at which he supervised a patient.

"We sat down and listened to this singer and Jimmie said to me, 'Charlie, the bottle'. So I takes him out and opens his breeks and hold the bottle, but nothing comes. So I button up his breeks again and back we go, quiet, into the concert. Well, we were hardly settled down and listening to the next turn when Jimmie nudges me again and says, 'Charlie, the bottle'. So out we go again, quietly, and I open his breeks and hold the bottle and wait; but nothing comes. So I button up his breeks again and back we go to the concert."

(I realised that his story was in the tradition of the Scottish ballads. There was the same simplicity, the stark facts, the use of direct speech, the repetition of the same words; and a story to tell.)

"Well, hardly had we sat down again listening when old Jimmie nudges me and says, 'Charlie, the bottle'. So out we goes and I opens up his breeks and hold the bottle and wait but nothing comes and back we go into the concert.

"In a wee while he nudges me again. 'Charlie,' he says, 'Charlie!' I says, 'Aye?' He says, 'Charlie, I've done it in my breeks'."

They told me about the grounds of the hospital where they took the patients for walks. "There's a peacock walks about free in the grounds," one of the boys told me. "Have you ever **seen** a peacock?"

I said yes, I'd seen a peacock.

He said, "Yes, but have you ever really looked at a peacock?"

While I was hesitating he continued, "This peacock, it spreads out its feathers like a fan and the feathers are full of wee circles of green and blue and brown. Amazing."

Helping old men in a mental hospital had converted (temporarily, at any rate) two difficult youngsters into relaxed, friendly, more observant and articulate beings. Other schools have made similar discoveries.

Most of the year staff had similar stories to tell of pupils who dropped their hostility to adults and became friendly and trusting. There were others, already launched on a career of crime, who began to have misgivings about their anti-social activities but nevertheless persisted in them. Individually they would discuss those activities in a calm, open manner, telling the year master or year mistress about the pressures forcing them this way and that; but surrounded by their gang they would display a cold, biting hostility to the year masters which gave no indication of the relaxed, friendly spirit of their talks together, perhaps only the previous day. It was no doubt partly a front, set up to reassure the gang that the pupil hadn't gone soft; but it was frequently more than that. Some pupils wondered if, after all, the "hard men" weren't right, who rejected every advance by a year master; they suspected themselves of having been taken in too easily by the friendliness of the year master, the cup of coffee, the use of the first name. Their suspicions would be confirmed when they saw the year master emerging from the staffroom chatting affably to another teacher who had frequently belted that pupil. I think they doubted us all.

There is the story about a class who were asked to write a composition about the police. One boy wrote, "The police is bastards" and left it at that; not another word on the page. The school and the police thereupon co-operated in an exercise in public relations. The boy was taken to police headquarters, shown the nature of their work, entertained in the canteen, and taken out in a car. Back in school he was given another chance to write his essay. He wrote, "The police is cunning bastards." In Summerhill there were several pupils, perhaps more than we liked to imagine, who were proof against kindness and cups of coffee, and retained their suspicion of the year masters, regarding them as merely a more insidious type of prefect of the establishment.

I can't get away from the nagging thought that they were right. Was all that we were doing just the soft-sell, disarming their suspicions in order the more smoothly to help the present social and educational system to work? Were we, with subtle flattery, offering certificates, testimonials for jobs, public approval in the same way as Whitehall offers honours, promotions, jobs in nationalised industry, dinner parties, foreign travel, all the kingdoms of the world and the glory of them. ("All these things will I give thee, if thou wilt fall down and worship me.") Some of these sullen suspicious pupils of ours were the real freedom fighters, incorruptible like John MacLean or Che Guevara.

Some difficult decisions await to be made by us teachers. Those who follow the uncompromising honesty of John MacLean will be sacked, and there's no future, no immediate future in that for the teacher and his wife and family. The best that most of us can do is to make our compromises where possible but never to deceive ourselves into thinking that we are free agents acting on behalf of the pupils when in fact we are kept servants acting on behalf of our paymasters. Even within that limit there is still much that we can do to alleviate suffering, to patch up and smooth over — activities not to be sneered at. I look back at a creditable list of achievement of Summerhill's year staff and other liberal-minded teachers along these lines. A year master took a group of a dozen boys for a weekend on the hills. In the evening, in the youth hostel, when they were relaxing after suppertime, he noticed that they were passing round souvenirs and discussing them — horn spoons and curios made of deer's antlers, tartan trinkets, granite paperweights, embroidered bookmarkers. Aberdeen children are notoriously eager to bring home presents for their parents and friends after even a weekend excursion. They had got these presents in Braemar where they had stopped for half an hour's break after the 60-miles' journey from Aberdeen. But no, they admitted reluctantly, they hadn't paid for them. The year master put to them the shopkeeper's point of view. With the ready generosity of children they expressed their sympathy for him; they hadn't looked at it that way, and they agreed to hand the souvenirs back when they reached Braemar on their return journey. When he stopped the bus a hundred yards short of the shop their courage began to fail them and they asked him to accompany them. He refused; this was a confronta-tion, he said, that they would have to enter upon alone. So they went, and handed back the souvenirs and said they were sorry. When they were all back in the bus the teacher went on his own to see the shopkeeper. The shopkeeper said he had no wish to involve the police. He had noticed that the articles had disappeared but when many people were wandering round the shop it was difficult to watch over everything. He understood the temptations that children are up against and thanked the teacher for the part he had played.

I mention this incident because I feel the teacher handled it with professional distinction. The goods were returned, the shopkeeper was entirely satisfied, the pupils' respect for the bravado-cunning of the shoplifters had been diluted with compassion.

We've been told that we are delaying the revolution; it will come quicker through the action of the other schools that belt pupils who steal trinkets. Maybe it's true. Maybe we're the real conmen, inducing the pupils to act with sympathy and understanding and trust, and implying that these are the qualities that permeate the adult world. The teachers with the leather belts, it is said, are the realists, preparing pupils for life as it really is, in the adult world. "Unrealistic" was the emotive adjective frequently thrown at us. We made every concession to the realists, for example, cramming pupils for examinations with the best of them. But there comes a point where there is nothing else you can do than follow your own leading. If compassion is unrealistic in the modern world, well, we were content to be unrealistic.

There was a girl of 15 who had been before the juvenile court for stealing. Teachers frequently complained about her outbursts of bad temper. She was said to be uncontrollable. Some of the class teachers were angry with the year-mistress for failing to control her. She truanted, roved about the corridors, occasionally throwing open a room door to shout an obscenity into the classroom and then take to her heels, hoping to enjoy the thrill and attention of pursuit. She "skulked" in the lavatories, smoking. One day somebody searching for her reported her to be in the lavatory, "probably smoking". But she was ill and she was taken to the school clinic. The deputy head phoned the girl's doctor and he said to take her home. But there was nobody at home and we didn't want to leave her there all day alone. We phoned her mother at her place of work but she was unwilling to leave her work. We phoned the works manager who understood the situation and was very helpful. He said he'd send the mother home and assure her that, even if she had to be off for several days looking after her daughter, she wouldn't lose her job. Finally, we took the girl home and suggested that she call the doctor. But next morning the girl walked to school again, vomiting blood on the way, and we got her a hospital appointment and she was taken into hospital.

Another girl ran away from home several times but usually emerged in the periphery of the school as if wanting to be caught and was easily persuaded into coming into the school for a cup of coffee. Because of a record of stealing she was sent to a succession of approved schools, latterly called List D schools, and, because she ran away from these, she was then sent to a borstal. Later, for further offences, she was sent to prison. She was one of the people whom I think we could have helped; perhaps we might even have helped her to sidestep a future of borstal and prison. But the local authority wouldn't let us. They said she "needed more discipline". It was sometimes suggested that our "soft" attitude towards her confirmed her in a career of crime.

There were other pupils from more normal home backgrounds, lively, independent-minded youngsters who, I believe, would have been no problem at all in a less-authoritarian system. But teachers enforced upon them a system of knowledge which the external authority enforces upon the teachers and the pupils reacted at first angrily and latterly in revolt. "They needed more discipline," said the authorities. Maybe this book will help the world outside the closed circle of educationists to start enquiring into the nature of the educationists' arguments. When some of these pupils refuse to memorise notes on rainfall in Australia, the authorities look around for ways of compelling them. When the pupils in exasperation hit out, they are described as recalcitrant and they are punished. That is called disciplining them. It's not only the dramatic effect of this jackboot policy on the young, more ardent spirits that is regrettable. There is also the effect on a large number of pupils, easy-going and friendly, who want to be in friendly association with us but who now come to their own conclusions about the unreasonableness of authority and settle into a vague attitude of passive resistance. Adults, they generalise, are mostly unreasonable. And this attitude is fortified when they discuss things at home and the parents support the teachers.

The school's main type of activities were divided from one another as by bulkheads in a ship. There were the year staff concerned that the pupils should be happy, stable, confident. They were thinking of the social development of the pupils, and their individual development as all-round people. Many other members of the staff played an important part in this area of school work; they were teachers rather than instructors, not limiting their interest in the pupil to instruction in their own specialty. Some of these teachers were the best type out of the old dispensation. Like many of the parents they believed in discipline, corporal punishment (but didn't use it much), short hair, tidiness, school uniform, the outward signs of respect in addressing a teacher, compliance with orders, maintaining a distance between teacher and pupil. Within these prescriptions they were humane, humorous, sympathetic people. Some of the technical teachers in particular belonged to this group.

There was orderliness in their workshops but the pupils felt also the security of friendliness — they have told me so. They would give up their free time ungrudgingly to help pupils who sought help; when the pupils were leaving school they went to much trouble to place them in congenial employment. They were concerned for the welfare of the pupils. They were not clock-watchers; they gave up evenings, weekends, part of their holidays to the supervision of pupil activities. They associated themselves with the school and identified themselves with its interests. They were part of the north-east tradition. They were hard-working, conscientious, contented, good neighbours, entering fully into the community life, producing sterling work. They provided the consistency and the cement which held society together, the continuing culture and framework of ideas in which I grew up and which we all accepted because they were there like sunshine and rain and the other things that made up our environment. They didn't enquire much into the nature of this society. In times when life didn't alter much from one generation to the next, people like these provided stability. But in times of rapid change and growing enquiry, some of their virtues block changes, obstruct the free flowing of the stream and build up back pressures. And that is what happened in the school. Like the best kind of conservatives they fought to retain not only the virtues which they esteemed but also the framework they knew, because they thought that it was the only structure within which these virtues could flourish or, indeed, survive. They resisted change and suspected those who were helping to bring it about. That is why they sided, reluctantly I sometimes thought, with the rigorous authoritarians who wanted to bring back an army discipline and the right to belt pupils of all ages. I could have worked with these moderate conservatives. A staff of nearly a hundred should be able to contain a wid'h of opinion, provided there is a basic agreement on a general attitude of friendliness towards the pupils; and these teachers·continued to treat the pupils, and be treated by most of the pupils, as friends. Sometimes the compromise was difficult but I felt it was worth making. But when the authoritarians began to exercise pressure on these moderates, bringing them into their camp, compromise was no longer possible. One of the activities of the school (the maintenance of friendly relations with all pupils and helping them to develop into mature, confident, happy adults) was in jeopardy.

But at no time was that seen to be the main purpose and activity of Summerhill Academy (or of any Scottish state school). The main purpose is working for the Scottish Certificate of Education examinations. An advertisement inviting applications for the post of head teacher of James Gillespie's High School in Edinburgh (a state school), said that "In SI and SII the pupils are following a common course but in SIII to SVI all work is geared towards presentation in the

Scottish Certificate of Education examinations". This is why the traditional system of education in Scotland has been so little affected by the introduction of comprehensive education. That Edinburgh school's brutally honest statement shows how little thought is given to the pupils who aren't likely to pass any of the examinations and how little thought is given to any activity which is not a mark-earning activity.

It is a desolating experience to look out on a large, well-equipped, busy school and realise that almost all its work and resources are dedicated to this purpose. Memorising information — that's about all it comes to. It's a waste of time and energy and money on a colossal scale. Here I am up against it in this book. For who will believe that the educational priesthood is mistaken in the reverence expressed in their punctilious observance of the rituals of this national religion? You can get a hearing if you indict instances of inefficiency here or injustice there; but if you indict a large area of our national life and say it is folly, what chance have you against the high priests and their ready access to the media?

The machinery is so big and complicated that it is beyond the wit of an individual human being to intervene; the machine has taken over. The examination machine, which is a machine to make people memorise information, gets all the publicity and its policy is promoted widely until nearly all the parents regard the examination system as the same thing as education. The nature of this system is publicised and commended in television programmes on Brain of Britain, University Challenge, Top of the Form, and endless quizzes. Education is memorising information, and there's the beginning and the end of it.

The unreality is so obvious and on so large a scale and its propaganda so brazen that I'd have thought a civilisation of free men and women would have enquired into it long ago. On the one hand there is the immediate world of our Aberdeen background — rows at home, oil, cost of living, entertainment, fish, Pittodrie football, violence, change. On the other hand are the examination questions on ciliated epithelium, the oxygen consumption of the humming bird at rest, feeding heterotrophically, gibberellic acid, the egg, relations between India and Pakistan, the development of the curved surface of a truncated cylinder, transhumance, progesterone, nitrosomonas, coleoptiles, laterite, chernozem, Stolypin's reforms, Carl Peters, the reforms in the Penal Code in the 1820s, education in 1868. It is not merely the ragbag of disconnected pieces of information that the children must carry on their backs. There is the unnatural demand to have all the mark-scoring details (for example on a question about the relations between India and Pakistan) immediately available on the date of the examination.

The examiners don't know where they are going or where their examination questions are leading the students. But they are skilful in hiding,behind a fog of words, this lack of a clearly seen educational purpose. In 1972 the draft proposals of the Scottish Certificate of Education Examination Board for an "alternative" "O" grade examination in geography gave advice which was less than illuminating. It was necessary (said their official document) "to point, albeit implicitly, towards certain basic questions inherent in the subject matter in the expectation that these questions may themselves guide teacher and pupil enquiry, through the medium of geographical study, towards recognisable educational objectives".

Maybe this unrelatedness of what is taught in school to how life is lived is due to excessive specialisation. Unsuccessful efforts have been made to relate the two. Edinburgh University provided lectures in moral philosophy for their first-year medical students, but the lecturers did not deal with the problems that students or doctors would find thrown at them to solve on their own as best they could; the lecturers dealt with what Aristotle and Hegel and Kant said. They were part of the tradition that learning means memorising information for examinations, and learning about philosophy means memorising what Aristotle and Hegel and Kant said. As simple as that. Similarly chemistry at a cookery college has less to do with cooking than one might have hoped. The heads of the cookery colleges want to raise the prestige of their profession andtheybelieve the way to do it is to have less and less to do with the vulgar operations of cooking a meal and more with chemical formulae. This would be admirable if the chemistry was closely related to cooking, but it isn't — any more than Hegel's writings are closely related by moral philosophers to the problems that medical students will have to try and solve. But it is comforting to remember that Louis Pasteur was keen to relate his talents to ordinary life, beer-making and vine-growing, as well as to the cure of bacterial diseases.

This memorising of information against the great day puts a strain on the teacher and the children. As long as only a small minority of children were put through these hoops, the circus masters got by without too much publicity. The unwilling performers or the poor performers left the school. But when all were compelled to stay on and hoop-training became obligatory, there was trouble. Unwillingness or inability to do the tricks was regarded as a defect of character. This charge of a defect of character was regarded as proved when children, humiliated by their failure, snarled at the ringmaster as he cracked his whip. It is a strain also on the parents. When parents accept an invitation to meet the staff of secondary schools to hear how their children are progressing, almost the whole evening is given over to a discussion of examination prospects. Tom's French has gone up but his maths has gone down and he'll need to work harder at his history It might be a good idea to drop art in order to increase his chances of getting history. These evening sessions have a pervasive unreality about them. Teachers, parents and children have got into a nightmare road from which there is no turning. A friend of mine, studying for a year in Toronto, was in a small car in a long, straight thoroughfare, and closely in front of a speeding fire engine. He had to drive so fast that there wasn't time to slow down to turn off and get out of the way of the following fire engine. These parents' meetings have the same mixture of comedy and nightmare, everybody being chased by the juggernaut of the examination system. There's something superficially farcical and profoundly disturbing in watching all these trustful and worried parents wandering round from one teacher to another, holding pieces of paper on which they write William's class mark in English (30 per cent) and in art (67 per cent). Scene two is later that evening in William's bedroom where he is confronted by two distraught parents brandishing this piece of paper like a summary of the evidence against him, and the trial begins.

Few things do so much to widen the gap between parents and children as that piece of paper does. In the twilight of traditional religion a new controlling faith has taken hold of men's minds, an unquestioning faith in the examination system. The priests of this cult, knowing that they hold the child's future in their hands, are inexorable in the demands they make on the parents, and control the parents' attitudes to their child. It is as difficult to persuade a parent to ignore the demands of the educational high priests as it would have been to persuade Abraham that he didn't have to contemplate the sacrifice of his son.

It is this inaccessibility to reason, an ineluctable quality in the educationists confirmed in their defence of the system, that is disturbing. They will sacrifice their children rather than sacrifice their examination questions. I think there is a deep, primeval fear, a feeling that if the fortifications of the examination system are breached, they will be exposed to who knows what forces of darkness. When the Scottish teachers, in their battle to get better pay, threatened to boycott the external examinations for that year, the vice-chairman of the Examination Board said, "This is the next inevitable step in the lurch to total anarchy. If the teachers really want to wreck the country, this is the way for them to do so." And another member of the board said, "To the kids concerned it will be much more final than, say, turning off the water supply."

There is something unnerving about this panic, as of a primitive people deprived of their idols. Without them they cannot live. It would be more possible to do without water than without the examinations. When I try to show parents that we can educate their children better without the examinations, the vehemence of their answers indicates a deep-seated fear. I have a feeling of fear when I encounter this irrationality, the kind of unco feeling that the Scottish kirk minister in

John Buchan's **Witchwood** felt when he saw his most respectable
parishioners in a witches' coven.

It is in situations like these that you realise that some educational
problems are not amenable to solution by normal, rational
discussion. They are too deep-seated for that. We need the wisdom
acquired by anthropology and archaeology and social psychiatry if
we are going to assuage these irrational fears. This is foggy country,
not the sunny uplands. Maybe our anthropologists and psychiatrists
are not yet equal to the assignment. Maybe we should follow the
example of Don Revie who got an old gypsy to remove the spell from
Leeds football ground at Elland Road.

A critic, reading this chapter, asked, "What about examinations for
doctors, architects, ships' officers?" Few people would oppose
examinations where the purpose is to measure the student's
knowledge and test his skills. The public has to be guarded against an
ignorant doctor or architect or ship's officer. But these professions
and many others require also qualities that are not measured by
examinations. The assessment of human ability is a study which is
still in its infancy. Examination passes in school sometimes give a
good indication of future success. Sometimes pupils who fail the
examinations succeed later. An assessment given by an experienced
teacher who knew the student well, although still fallible, could be
wider-ranging, more sophisticated. Those who emphasise the
objectivity of the external examination imply that teachers aren't to
be relied on. An insurance company can rely on a doctor to give an
objective report on a client who wishes to insure his life, but not on a
teacher to give an objective report on a student who has applied for a
job with the insurance company. That's the implication.

At Summerhill the staff were engaged on two activities, the welfare
of the pupils and helping them to pass examinations. The second was
far and away the major activity. As the religious year is divided up by
the minor and major observances of religious festivals (Epiphany,
All Saints, Easter and Christmas), so the educational year has fixed
times for its rituals. In Scotland's education, the New Year begins at
the end of August. At the end of November the first diet of worship
takes place, the First Preliminary Examinations. At the end of
January the Second Preliminary Examinations take place. It is on
the basis of these results that forecasts are made to the Examination
Board of what the pupils will achieve in the actual examinations. The
climax of the year is the holding of the examinations in April and May.
The school year doesn't end until the end of June and there are several
weeks of anti-climax (like the days after Christmas in the religious
year), when the senior classes disintegrate. But in between these
major festivals are numerous smaller observances strictly
mandatory on the teachers.

In the midst of real problems amounting to a crisis of society it is eery to sit in a school richly equipped to solve unreal problems and energetically engaged in that activity. In our youth we assume that teachers are as concerned to solve educational problems as a motor mechanic is to get a car engine running smoothly. In education it's not like that at all, and when I talked to friends of mine in other spheres of activity, they tell me that they also spent their time on unreality and that the people who direct their activities are not innovators. An article in the **British Medical Journal** said that you don't get papers published unless your findings are in agreement with the views of the ruling orthodoxy. I think this is largely economic; no professor or director or manager is kindly disposed towards an idea which may threaten his prestige and in due course his pay. But it is also due to human fatigue. Matthew Arnold, a school inspector, wrote:

> And each day brings its petty dust
>   Our soon-choked souls to fill,
> And we forget because we must
>   And not because we will.

The chapter on his father, Thomas Arnold of Rugby, in Lytton Strachey's **Great Victorians**, throws some light on the nature of traditional educational endeavour. For Arnold the main props of education were Latin, Greek and the Bible, and he gave much earnest enquiry into a biblical problem that troubled him. In II Chronicles 11: 20, it says that the mother of Abijah, King of Judah, was Maachah the daughter of Absalom, but in II Chronicles 13: 2, it says that his mother was Michaiah, the daughter of Uriel of Gibeah. This confusion over Abijah's parentage was to Arnold a serious matter. I believe that a future generation will view most of the laborious educational research of today in the same light as we view Arnold's concern over a biblical contradiction.

Most of the work carried out by teachers and pupils in Summerhill was as remote from our problems as research into Abijah's parentage. The form of examination questions (to which the whole exercise was directed) hadn't changed in a hundred years. Then it had been the dimensions of the ark or Solomon's temple, or the weight of Goliath's spear. A Victorian educationist justified these questions by declaring that, "If I found the children acquainted with the minutiae, I inferred a general knowledge of scriptural truth." I expect the examiners (in so far as they pause to consider the purpose of their activities) would justify in the same way today's emphasis on mark-earning details.

I signed requisitions in triplicate and authorised the expenditure of large sums of money to buy bigger and better and more expensive sets of detail-crammed books to meet the latest examination orthodoxy. The new maths was coming under fire from the new, new maths. One subject after another switched from the traditionaı examination paper to what was called the alternative examination paper and, as the traditional paper was superseded, thousands of pounds' worth of textbooks throughout the country became obsolete and publishers did well out of this new captive market, which was expanding, as more and more industrialists were persuaded to demand examination certificates from pupils leaving school. There was little basic difference between the traditional books and questions and the new, alternative books and questions. It is a recurrent historical pattern which the French summarised in their saying, "The more it changes, the more it remains the same thing." A semblance of modernity was produced by the purchase of very expensive new machinery. Audio and visual aids, they were called. Blackboard work was supplemented by overhead projections, textbooks were supplemented by radio. There were strip projectors and photocopiers. Insurance companies insisted that special lockfast rooms be provided for the security of this expensive equipment, and a system of booking out and booking in and transport to the classrooms of this equipment had to be organised. Some teachers found the drill so time-consuming that they didn't bother to use the equipment. Anyway pupils accustomed to wide screens in the cinemas and colour television at home soon found the audio and visual aids as uninteresting as the textbooks. And it was the old wine that was coming now in the new bottles, and they knew the taste of the old wine and recognised it.

There was remarkable ingenuity displayed in the effort to make the latest in equipment serve the old requirements. It was as if Arnold of Rugby had got a large grant from the Department of Education and Science to use carbon 14 to try and settle the vexed question of Abijah's parentage. Large sums of money were poured uncritically into what was called educational research, conferences were held, teachers were released for in-service courses, specialised new periodicals were required for the libraries, exhibitions of the latest equipment toured the country. All very brash and modern and with-it. "The introduction of new ideas," it was called. Resources centres were set up and teachers cajoled to visit them. Committees on specialist subjects were set up both centrally and locally and we had to read a succession of their reports as they appeared and we were besought to attend local meetings to discuss the reports. Teachers staggered from a conference on computers to a conference on what was called "minority time" (time spent on non-examinable subjects) and their eyes became more and more glazed.

And it was all a great weariness and vexation of spirit, the desperate flicker of a decaying system incapable of self-criticism and self-renewal. The vital question — in our brief time between two eternities are we really spending our children's schooldays to the best advantage? — was never allowed to surface. We'll never solve the mounting problems of education until we face this question. In nearly every school in the country the resolute refusal to contemplate it, like a monastery's refusal to contemplate sex, causes continuing troubles. They go growling and forever padding around like caged beasts, occasionally breaking out and mauling somebody, leaving destruction behind them. Few things better illustrate the failure and unreality of the educational system than does the wilful blindness of the educationists to the deep causes of their own troubles. What a complex of emotions a secondary school is. There are teachers of physical education and of technical subjects who resent being regarded as less than **real** teachers, not like teachers of mathematics for example, and compensate for pay differentials operating against them by asserting themselves the more aggressively in the class-room. There are teachers with honours degrees who dislike the new opportunities of promotion offered to "ordinary" graduates. There are heads of departments who are suspicious of the year masters who get the same responsibility payments as they do, and feel that it is unfair that year masters should spend half an hour in friendly discussion with a recalcitrant pupil, drinking coffee, while the heads of departments are enduring the heat and burden of the day. There was a feeling amongst these heads of departments that we should close the ranks against the disturbers of the peace. In the R.A.F. in South Africa in 1943 we were requested not to fraternise with the natives; it was implied that this was letting the side down. In the face of the stranger, the potential enemy, the alien, there was the same appeal to esprit de corps in the staff. Some teachers who got on badly with pupils resented teachers who got on well with the same pupils. There were attendance officers who said that year masters had no right to call at pupils' homes to discuss the pupils with the parents; that was the attendance officer's job. Some of these attendance officers, dressed in uniform, and in a little brief authority, shouted at the parents and were disturbed at the friendly welcome accorded by the parents to the year masters (who didn't shout). I sympathised with the attendance officers, who found a tradition crumbling under their feet. Not their fault but they had been brought up in a tradition dating much farther back than Shakespeare but noted by him, the tradition of the insolence of office. And similarly, some teachers who had been in manual work and who had made it to the university and thereby advanced in status, were non-plussed at seeing their hard-earned status carelessly ceded, like a fortress, by teachers who fraternised on easy and equal terms with impertinent working-class recalcitrants. It is curious how caste, status, lays hold of the adult mind.

In the staff, deep division underlay what seemed to be political solidarity. We had one communist, an authoritarian, honest, humane, hostile to the "difficult" pupils, accepting the curriculum without question, allying himself to the opinions of the majority of the staff; outside politics, uncritical of the status quo, unenquiring. We had another communist, libertarian, honest and humane, friendly to the "difficult" pupils, critical of the curriculum, never calculating, selfless, independent of majority opinion, intellectually venture-some. Their common membership of the Communist Party suggested the impermanence of human associations, the brittle, tentative nature of what seemed to be enduring, monolithic associations regimented by "whips" and fearful of any disclosure of fundamental differences. I think one of the gains made by the present generation is that they are less fearful of facing disquieting facts, readier to abandon prepared positions if the new positions are based on a more comprehensive synthesis, more prepared to give up the comforting appearance of unity for the sometimes desolate reality of what seemed to be irreconcilable facts. It is as if the walls of the compartments are dissolving and new associations emerging. I found the same division in the Catholic Church as I found in the Communist Party. A local priest attacked the work we were doing in the school, but the local branch of the Newman Society defended it. I think we are entering into a new world where the old self-appointed law-givers are losing their credibility and people are thinking out their own thoughts and forming their own allegiances without reference to them. Soon it may no longer be a question of being Communist or Catholic, or of bending one's thought to discover which orthodoxy one can fit into with the least distortion or discomfort. We are beginning to escape from a prison of words in which the human spirit has been cooped up for so long. We are looking at the words and discovering that they are not the immutable realities we had been brought up to believe. Words are merely noises in the throat or marks on paper; as evanescent as that. Some were helpful in their time. We leave them behind like crutches and walk uncertainly but with a new hope and a vague surmise into a new era.

Every year in the school the attitudes depart farther and farther from the previously accepted and enduring norm. Because the teachers have been trained in static institutions, they are not prepared for the dynamic situation of the classroom. Every year there are more and more pupils who shout back at a teacher in the same tone as the teacher used towards them.

"Hey, Brown," shouts the teacher, "stop talking."

"Hey, Smith," shouts the pupil, "you're not going to talk to me like that, or I'll talk to you in the same way."

The growing resistance reinforces itself. Pupils driven to distraction by the enforced inactivity and the dullness of the lessons have a shorter threshold of tolerance and when the aggression of the teacher is added to the boredom of the lesson, they lash out. The prowling beasts rattle the bars, and the frightened keepers demand "more discipline", more whips, stronger cages.

The bars at some of the other comprehensives rattled louder than those at Summerhill, but it was the noise at Summerhill that got the newspaper publicity.

Gradually and later I realised the full significance of what was happening when the pupil shouted back to the teacher, "Hey, Smith." It is part of a world movement. In Chile and the Dominican Republic, peasants learning to read were beginning to think their own thoughts and were refusing to be cowed. In an article about Paulo Freire, the magazine of the Christian Education Movement, **Learning for Living**, said that there was an awakening of awareness in which a human being recognises himself as a person, an active subject rather than a passive object; aware that he can improve his own situation and, acting with others, change society and make life truly human. There is a new-found dignity and courage. I began to realise not only that our pupil Willie Brown and others like him were standing shoulder to shoulder with peasants of the New World, but also that Scottish education was standing shoulder to shoulder with the oppressive regimes of Chile and Dominica. For all these long centuries the smoking flax of the human spirit downtrodden, has refused to be quenched. Sporadic outbursts like the revolt of the Spartacists have been savagely extinguished, but the struggle continues. The bruised reed is not broken and the smoking flax is not quenched. Paulo Freire is on to something vital here, the core of what is called the problem of revolt if it is in the adult world, and recalcitrance if it is in the schools. People have fought battles for bread and physical comfort but the human spirit needs more than that. People need to abandon the stooping gait and walk tall; they have the ability to cope with their problems of living. If a civilisation does not give them that, no matter what their wages or fringe benefits or standard of living, it denies them the vital thing, the essential vitamins without which their growth is stunted and their lives unsatisfactory; and that society is a tyranny. Because it denies this to its young people, Scottish education is a tyranny.

It is in keeping with a tyranny that it should seek to stigmatise any revolt as a crime. Here again we are at the core of the present enquiry into the nature of our society. Questions are being asked more frequently now about the facts behind indoctrination. Why was obedience to THE LAW invested with such emotive, religious feeling? It is only a society unsure of its ability to provide intelligent reasons for support of the law that seeks to envelop the law in an aura of mystical cloud. Gradually we begin to blow away the clouds of emotion that surround some words and to realise that words like law and crime and sacred are frequently totems by which the prefects of a society warn off trespassers. A Dominican peasant who hits back is a terrorist; an Aberdeen pupil who shouts back is a recalcitrant, both (we are told) should be punished. But it's now no longer possible to get away with the brandishing of words like terrorist and recalcitrant. Education may play the vital part in the revolution; we won't need gelignite if our classrooms are infiltrated with pupils asking questions. The incantations of the newspaper leader-writers lose their spell under these insistent questions. We no longer shiver at the denunciations of Judge Cocklecarrot; we begin a fuller enquiry into what the law has been up to while it was posturing as an agent in our defence. Our Scottish society is seen to be at a much earlier stage of development, much more of a witch-doctoring mind-control than it has encouraged us to guess. Freire says that education is either liberation or domesticisation. And that is what the row at Summerhill was about. We were trying to introduce liberation into a state system which historically is based on domestication.

Freire says that any situation which hinders somebody's "pursuit of self-affirmation" is one of oppression, any situation which prevents people or pupils acquiring "social literacy" and the confidence in their own ability (their intelligence and understanding and goodwill and energy) to struggle for and achieve a more human life. I found that this statement helped awkward parts of the jigsaw to fit together. It explained the falling away of the Labour Party. The Labour Party helped to achieve rights and better conditions, but when it moved into a different sphere and introduced comprehensive education, it had not clearly enough considered what education is really about and therefore its comprehensive education became as much an oppressive thing as the system it might have replaced; its education remained one in which the teacher places "quantities of information or knowledge in his students' empty safe deposit heads so that they can store, file and repay it as examination questions on demand". Basically it means that the Labour Party undervalues the pupils' capacity in general, and in particular their capacity to work out on their own a better kind of society.

There's another puzzle that Freire's explanation helped to solve. Often at meetings people have heckled me about how we are to bring in social and educational change. They said that you couldn't have an educational change unless you had political power. But any people whom you put into Parliament now will have been brought up within the traditional indoctrination of the educational system and therefore not only predisposed to retain the educational system but, like the Labour Party, eager to extend it more widely (over the children of working-class parents). So where do we begin?

The answer is, I think, that you begin with the teachers. Education, as Freire said, is not neutral. Either you believe that only the minority are intelligent and have to be trained to run society, or you believe that the majority are more intelligent than the present schools are prepared to admit, in which case you seek to operate a really comprehensive system of education in which you prepare all pupils to take a full active part in working out what kind of society they want and in bringing that society into being. This is, I think, one of the big shifts in opinion in our time — the final admission that we've got as far as we're likely to get with the present system of government by narrowly trained politicians whose objectives are limited to material gains for the voters. We're now like an African people who say to even the kindest of paternalistic colonial administrators, "Well, thank you very much, and we'll take over from now, even if it means that for the sake of freedom to run our own country ourselves, we have for a time fewer material benefits." It is a new phase in the development of human society; the teachers take over the initiative from the politicians in order that the majority can be involved in running the country. It's the next step towards a much wider devolution of power, the next step towards democracy.

Education, the preparation of a child for living in the adult world, and therefore for shaping that world in the way he wants to shape it, is not neutral; it is clearly political. The traditionalists who say they want to keep it neutral are not, in fact, neutral; their neutrality means preserving the advantages and the values of the minority. Thus the change I'm envisaging is not the making of a neutral system into a political system; it is ending an educational system which brings up pupils to accept and believe in the elite, it is setting the pupils free from the bondage of intellectual tyranny now imposed on them by servants of the elite in the interests of the elite. (And it is interesting that just as a growing number of educationists are working to rescue the educational system from its present function of being a supportive part of the present social system, so some theologians are working to rescue the religious system from the same function.)

Thus it is not surprising that Summerhill was a battleground. Uniformed attendance officers, like military police, checked up on the truants, the personnel absent without leave. Psychological casualties were given treatment and returned to the firing-line; they were considered cured if they attended regularly and were quiet in the classroom. The juvenile courts which tried the sinners were replaced by the children's hearings which were intended to help rather than punish. The children's hearings were (like Summerhill) typical institutions of a society in transition, a society midway between two worlds. The well-intentioned adults who supervised these hearings found it difficult to know what to do. If they let the sinners off too lightly they were called **soft;** if they condemned them too readily to an approved school, they were being too punitive. Part of the dilemma appeared to be solved when the approved schools had their names changed to List D schools, and the children were assured that this wasn't a punishment but the best treatment in their interest.

The Directors of Education, the Directors of Social Work, the members of children's hearings were pushed into some sort of make-do-and-mend, patching up, improvising activities. Any sort of safety pin and string methods to keep the establishment's trousers up and save it embarrassment. The education authorities would take the more severely disturbed pupils to a special school in the city of Aberdeen where they would be given remedial attention, so that, as the Aberdeen Director of Education wrote in his report, the pupils would be returned cured to their ordinary school in three weeks; and make way for a further batch of recalcitrants. As easy as that. The social work department would set up another school where bad boys and girls would go at times when they were most at risk, that is evenings, weekends and during the school holidays. It is a picture of Scotland in the seventies, still at the Heath Robinson stage of social education.

There is a mixture of comedy and pathos in this. An establishment in decay, like Hitler in the Berlin bunkers, desperately bidding the troops to hang on. The senior prefects of the Scottish establishment were handing down their orders; the present system must be made to work. Send in your orders for sandbags. Plug the holes. Summon conferences. The senior administrators have not only not been given an imaginative education which would have helped them to forsee disaster and work creatively, but are also least in touch with the conditions in the disaster areas. They have neither the imagination nor the first-hand experience and knowledge. The desperate tinkering with children's hearings was the same sort of thing as was happening in the examination sector. However futile and humorous the examinations might be, the examination system must be seen to work. So they altered the wording of some questions with meticulous care, discussed a fairer allocation of marks, and appointed a national committee (largely composed of technical experts) to plug up the holes in Scotland's "O" grade examinations. Anything rather than fundamental discussion about the nature of the educational system and the social system which were the real causes of the maladies. The legal-minded prefects would point out that fundamental rethinking is not in their brief. Like the private soldier, they would say they were not paid to think. Theirs not to reason why. In the school and outside of it we were faced with the prospect of an authoritarian system in a crisis which has not been foreseen and provided against in the Queen's Regulations.

Most of the headmasters I knew were influenced deeply in the Scottish tradition of headmastering. They worked very hard, arriving early and leaving late, and paying strict attention to detail. The construction of the timetable is the main event of their year and they pride themselves on being thoroughly knowledgeable on availability of teachers and accommodation and size of classes. They

have a detailed knowledge also of the succession of official forms
which precede and follow the great event of the year, the Scottish
Certificate of Education examinations. They are alert people, ready
to answer at a moment's notice any question on the running of their
business, the size of next year's intake, the degrees and qualifica-
tions of their staff, the number of pupils taking school dinners, looking
into classrooms to see that teachers are on their toes, reading and
annotating official reports, making liaison with employers, social
workers, police, child guidance clinics, universities. Their day is
divided into a multiplicity of details. I found many of them much more
knowledgeable than I was about the facts and figures of the schools.
They gave more time than I did to know the records of individual
pupils and they were obviously concerned for the pupils' future. In
many ways they were like good businessmen, taking their papers
home at night, maintaining good public relationships in an
enlightened manner, fitting easily into a rotary gathering. I wanted
to fault them but it was difficult to fault them; they had most of the
qualities, and most of their attitudes were moderate. They didn't like
corporal punishment but were against the abolition of corporal
punishment, they admitted the educational disadvantages of a system dominated by examinations but didn't see any way in which the
external examination system could be fundamentally altered; they
devoted their main energies to the pupils who were going on to higher
education but really did have the interests of the early leavers at
heart; they were disciplinarians (many of them church members)
but had an engaging sympathy for the sinners.

The directors of education were cast in a similar mould but their
area was more extensive, they were farther removed from pupils and
more concerned with maintaining good public relationships — with
teachers, employers, parents, members of education committees.
Most of them were happy if the machine committed to their trust
ticked over smoothly. And similarly the school inspectors were good
at their own subjects, occasionally communicating an infectious
enthusiasm for their subject along with particular skills, and ideas
culled from the schools they had visited. And most of these people,
when educational reform is in fashion, are moderately in favour of
educational reform; but nothing too much.

When I was removed from their ranks and had time to sit back and
survey a wider area, I realised that these key people in education
don't have the know-how which would unlock doors leading to an
ampler future for our children. They were, almost all of them, the
supporters, the maintainers of the existing order; they have never
envisaged any other. "The world is also stablished, that it can not
depart", says a Scottish metrical psalm. "To establish", says the
Oxford dictionary, is to "secure permanent acceptance for a custom,
a precedent, a belief, etc.''. These establishment figures, trained to

put into practice and to transmit the principles on which a stable society has been based, are up against it when faced with the problems of a society which has lost its stability. They have no precedents on which to base methods of restoring the balance. And it is of the nature of an established system that it trains its young people to be reverent to its own principles and beliefs and myths. They are not trained to be resourceful in an emergency. A relative of mine was appointed by his industrial firm to work full time on "future developments"; he had to know about research and inventions in other fields which in time might affect his firm, and advise them about these things so that they should foresee changes. There's nothing of this in education. It is assumed that the educational system, like the lathe or the bicycle, is so perfectly adapted to the demands made on it, that it will endure, largely unmodified, for ever.

There is no state school in the country that I know which has been permitted by its education committee to initiate basic experimental work. It is of the nature of our decaying society that it keeps its headmasters, and the company of directors and inspectors and ministry officials, so busy on the details of administration that they have no time to foresee the future and plan for it. When the ship goes down, they'll all be at their posts, filling in forms.

Chapter Five

THE VOICE
OF THE PEOPLE

I was naive in thinking that setting up school councils, "giving the pupils a measure of responsibility in the running of the school", would make any real difference to anything. Either you give them responsibility, which means accepting their decisions, or you tell them what to do. Anything else is a confidence trick and will fail.

The practice of consultation has had a long and dishonourable history. It's a manipulative measure adopted in the transition period between oligarchy and full democracy. When an oligarchy like the British Parliament wants to hold on to its power but feels that it's no longer respectable to say so, it employs the machinery called "consultation". "National Consultative Council" sounds good. It's a formula, a prescribed step in a stately minuet. The Secretary of State is duty bound to take into consideration the views expressed by this, that or the other consultative council. Then, the ritual having been duly observed, he makes up his mind in the old way.

An example of the trick in operation is given in the concluding chapter of John Buchan's story of adventure in Africa, **Prester John** (published in 1910). The white schoolmaster, writing home from Africa, says, "We have cleaned up all the kraals, and the chiefs are members of our county council and are as fond of hearing their own voices as an Aberdeen bailie." The paternal, amused note is inescapable. They are not so open about it nowadays; they pretend to take consultation seriously. But whether it's the story of devolution in the African states or the Aberdeen schools, the same blarney is used. They talk about gradualism, the limited exercise of responsibility, the evolution of power-sharing.

Aberdeen Education Committee asked its ten head teachers of comprehensives to report on the "present arrangements for consultation". One school said, "The council is a purely consultative body set up to create a channel by which views and suggestions of pupils could be conveyed to the headmaster." Another had year councils "consisting of representatives of each class in the year, elected subject to the approval of Register Teacher and Year Teacher; these meet regularly with Year Teacher as chairman, are free to discuss any relevant topics. Comments or suggestions are conveyed by Year Teacher to the Board of Studies". Another school didn't have a council but an "action committee", formed of four pupils from each year, four teachers, two year teachers, headmaster. "Action Committee" sounded good; but the report went on to say how limited the possibility of action was. "The Action Committee has authority to make decisions on social matters (e.g. dances, arrangements for hot or cold drinks at intervals, dealing with litter) but is confined, on general school policy, to discussing matters referred by headmaster."

Another school detailed the area to which council decisions were restricted — planning of school functions, disbursement of money raised in old age people's week.

Only Summerhill pretended to take its school council seriously, to make it mean something. Our staging was more elaborate. The voters' roll, the nomination of candidates, ballotting, declaration of the poll, the election of office bearers, keeping of minutes, signing of the minutes when their accuracy was agreed to, apologies for absence — we went through all the motions. But we never succeeded in gaining the interest of the majority of pupils. There were many useful discussions. Year after year the girls on the council appealed that girls should be allowed to wear trousers at school but the majority of the staff were against it. When the council maintained that, on winter mornings of snow and sleet, it would be more comfortable to wear trousers, a concession was made. Girls would be allowed to come to school in trousers, but must change into skirts when they arrived at the school. A reporter from the school newpaper interviewed the headmaster of a county school where the pupils were allowed to wear trousers; he said the reason was that many of their pupils came long distances and had to wait for buses. It is significant the way all of us had to scavenge for reasons to try and persuade a staff majority that girls should be allowed to wear trousers. For my own part I never saw clothes (or hair length) as major problems, but the majority of the staff didn't agree. They believed, they said, in the maintenance of standards, and to let girls wear trousers or boys grow their hair long was to abandon standards and lower the tone of the school. After council discussion, the pupils were allowed to wear jeans at their Christmas parties.

Another subject canvassed by the pupils was substituting soup for tea in the vending machines. The minute of the meeting said, "We will try the following soups — oxtail, chicken, pea and ham, in that order." Other subjects were putting a cover on the front of the pupils' notice board to prevent some pupils from tearing down the notices; organising the tuck shops; selling lemonade left over from Friday

night dances, dealing with boys who spat from the top of the stairs
down the central well, the provision of question boxes, comment on
school reports, parking bicycles, privileges for council members,
litter, bringing a local Member of Parliament to talk to senior pupils,
pupils who came in late, pupils' choice of records for some morning
assemblies, smoking, compulsory swimming, pupils not members of
the council who wore the council badge, taking transistors to school,
too much chlorine in the swimming pool, whether teachers should
have to queue for school dinners as the pupils did, damage to the
lavatories, the aggressiveness of monitors, whether "The Pigg" or
"The Facells" or "Mother Hubbard" should play at some of the
Friday dances, the use of form periods. They helped to raise money
for guide dogs for the blind. Every year the council raised £30 to
provide more food for a pupil in a Parsee school in Bombay.
Regularly the boy wrote to Summerhill acknowledging the gift and
describing his life. He studied English, Gujurati, Hindi, maths,
science, social studies, commerce, bookkeeping, scouting, P.T. and
art.

There were some advantages for the pupils in taking part in the
council. They became more articulate, they could declare their
membership when they applied for a job, and they discovered that
there are problems to which there are no neat, satisfactory solutions.
They discovered, for example, how difficult it is to choose councillors.
Some popular pupils stopped attending when they found that the
meetings could be dull; others because some pupils put pressure upon
them; others sensed the opposition of some members of the staff.

Pupils aiming at examination success are vulnerable. University
entrance depends partly on a headmaster's report, and that is
influenced by the reports of class teachers. Pupils who want to go to
the university have to watch their ps and qs. Too militant an involvement in the school council, or indeed any involvement in the school
council, may alienate a class teacher and affect his report. Once
again the school mirrors the adult world, where pupils' prospects
may be dimmed by their involvement in political activity. It is one
method by which an institution keeps its young turks in line,
"disciplines" them. This isn't the kind of adult world I was brought up
to believe in. I really did believe that most adults in responsible
positions acted responsibly and were proof against prejudice and
flattery and self-interest. This, I think, is the basic lie in our
education. People in authority aren't as good as the heroic myths tell
us. Watergate delivered a traumatic jolt to many simple and trusting
people. Even children are now realising that the pillars of society
aren't usually the steadfast characters they thought. The truth is
seeping through, even in the classroom. The reality of life is
beginning to be acknowledged. A Summerhill group were discussing
sex with a teacher. "Don't tell me you don't masturbate," the teacher

said to a boy. After an initial surprise the group entered on animated and happy discussion. A myth had been dispelled; many young people believe that they alone masturbate and that they alone therefore are miserable sinners. The teacher's question, like Watergate, uncovered the reality.

Thus some of the strains disrupting adult society, the realising of unsuspected facts, were present in the school. Successful pupils were becoming aware of constraints which some teachers were putting on them, and may have opted out of the council for that reason. Other pupils were regarded as using council membership largely as a distinction to put in a university application, like playing football for the school or canoeing. Some pupils who would have made excellent, hard-working and sturdily independent councillors were not elected. We discussed whether we should try in some way to co-opt such pupils. A school inspector asked me, "Do you find you get the best pupils on the council?" I replied, "Do you find you get the best people in Parliament?" He said, "I see what you mean." I told the pupils, when they felt discouraged, when the council was regarded as useless, or as a talking-shop, or as an elite, that their difficulties were also the difficulties of Parliament, the problems of democracy.

One of these is wider participation. To try and involve more pupils in council affairs we distributed through the school the minutes of every meeting and appealed to teachers to discuss these minutes with their class. But only a few teachers co-operated — partly because of examination pressures (the council, like art and drama and religion, was just a frill), partly because of the lack of warm liaison in a big school, partly because of ordinary human lethargy.

In spite of the difficulties and discouragements, I was heartened by the signs of enquiry and original thinking and independence that emerged and that gave us ground for believing that if only teachers could overcome their fear of "pupil power", the council would be successful. The council felt that boys were over-represented on it and devised means of restoring the balance. A pupil enquired what happened to the money that teachers charged pupils for lost jotters. There was a discussion on what to do about the pupils who didn't go out by the school gates but took a short cut across the grass and squeezed out through the railings. The councillors made it clear that they would have no part in identifying offenders. That was not the function of a school council, they said. I think they were right. There was a discussion on how to distinguish councillors, apart from giving them a badge to wear. Some said that acknowledged status would help them to operate more effectively. Several said they would refuse to accept any privileges since that was a form of bribery. As the Secretary of State had said when he opened Summerhill, these were young people groping for the truth.

More material things also engaged our pupils. School meals were frequently on the agenda. The minutes of one meeting reflected their detailed concentration on this subject.

"A majority of pupils would prefer milk and an orange (or apple) to a sweet, as well as a choice of something else.

"Most pupils prefer chips to potatoes.

"Second and fourth year want more choice and more food."

The cook in charge volunteered to appear before the council at their next meeting and she discussed the difficulties in fulfilling all the pupils' suggestions. She tried to be fair in distributing "seconds". The number of third- and fourth-year pupils taking dinners varied considerably from day to day and that made catering difficult. She asked if the council could help to keep numbers steady. She agreed to put some of their proposals into practice and explained clearly why others of their proposals were impracticable. It was an excellent lesson on human relations. The minute reads: "Mrs Gordon was thanked for attending the meeting. She was very helpful indeed. The council thought that Summerhill dinners are very good." And similarly the council were impressed by the readiness of Aberdeen's organiser of school meals to discuss dinners with them and to try and put their suggestions into practice.

Many circumstances prevented the council from being successful. Some were just the contrived awkwardnesses of living that circumvent the best-laid schemes. For example, one girl said she couldn't read out the minutes to her class at the form period because at that time she was having extra music. But the main cause was that many educationists didn't have the trust and tact and savoir-faire of the people who dealt with the school meals. School councils were coming into fashion; all the best schools were having them put in. It required much administrative skill to have a good-going council and yet prevent it from exercising any real power. Pupil power was not on the cards. One teacher, conscientious and concerned in social education, sent me a memorandum about the council's purpose. He suggested that teachers should help pupils to prepare a case; and he suggested that the things the council could tackle were theft, bullying, school meals, care of school property, social events, participation in social work. If the senior pupils favoured a council, could they win conviction for the idea of the council? Although the teacher had left-wing politics, I don't think he realised how closely his ideas about a council agreed with (and perhaps reflected) an English public school headmaster's ideas on the function of the prefects and a colonial governor's ideas on how to manipulate local chiefs.

The Summerhill School Council survived because of the loyalty of a few pupils who were unaffected by blame and criticism and gave up their time in the interests of the council, and the support of two teacher members elected by the staff who guided it with tact and understanding and explained the work to the rest of the staff. The school newspaper didn't survive. Its purpose was similar and complementary to that of the council — to reflect and give form to pupil opinion (as well as to keep all pupils informed of all school activities, to retell school gossip, and to provide a medium for prose, poetry and drawing). A newspaper reporter attended council meetings. The council discussed the titles for the newspaper proposed by pupils and staff. Some of the suggestions were ingenious. An old-established Scottish weekly paper is the **People's Journal**; one suggestion for the Summerhill newspaper was **Pupils' Journal.** Another was **Pop** (Pupils' Own Paper). Others were **Summerhill Flash, Flashback, Summerhill Saga, Summerhill Summary, Say** (Summerhill Academy Youth). **Say** became the title. When Mr William Ross, ex-Secretary of State for Scotland, opened the school as a comprehensive school eight years after its opening as a junior secondary school, the school newspaper gave on its front page two views of the opening. One said, "In the hall there were flowers all over the place, and seats on the stage for Mr Ross and other important guests. There was also a TV camera just in front of the stage. The Lord Provost of Aberdeen gave the first speech and he was followed by Mr Ross who talked mainly about education and urged children to speak up for themselves. After a prayer, Councillor Roy Pirie gave a speech which was about Mr Ross, and also a vote of thanks to the school."

The other view was this. "I think that the school opening was a load of rubbish. All they were trying to do was to impress this Mr Ross. What a stupid idea for flowers to be put all over the place. No matter where you went there were flowers. Now the school is opened, there are still no curtains up in some of the rooms and painting is still being done. What was all the fuss about anyway? The school has been up for years."

The pupils who produced the paper worked hard and with ingenuity, restyling the layout, combing for ideas, and publishing some good work. A poem about a summer day said:

> The water trinkled down the hill
> And only the sound of a bird
> In the distance singing a summer song
> The butterfly dancing on the grass
> Jumping to and fro
> And the world stood still
> In that warm summer sun.

Three first-year boys wrote about a teacher's car: "The seat on my

bicycle is softer than those in his car." A third-year girl contributed a
poem called "The Old Story":

> Have you got your homework?
> No, miss.
> Where is it?
> Home, miss.
> What's it doing there?
> Forgot it, miss.
> How?
> Didn't do it, miss.
> See me at 4.
> Yes, miss.

A news paragraph headed "Class Struggle" said that "the lower
classes (1, 2) are complaining at what they call the injustice of some
members of the upper classes in entering their year room and buying
their pies, leaving them hungry. 'Why don't they eat their own pies?'
they say." Pupils sent in news items about a week in New York, a
holiday with a married sister whose husband was with the army in
Germany, a pupil who brought his pet ferret to the school. Since
the paper was reproduced by photostat it was possible to publish, as
she wrote it, a paragraph written by a first-year girl , blot and all. She
wrote, "In my living room I have a thre peace sweet it is black and
red. I have an eletrick fire. I also have a television set and a radio
gramme. The carpet is red with flower designe on it. I also have
vinasen blinds. There is a picture above the fire place it is a picture of
horses."

A paragraph entitled "Pupils' Lib" said, "A new magazine called
Children's Rights has appeared in England. It prints a message from
the **Children's Angry Brigade** saying that pupils should use the same
method as industrial workers to get better conditions, including
sabotage. There should be a centre for truants where they could spend
their time in a more interesting and educative way than in school. If
you'd like to get a copy, hand in your name at the office and we'll see if
any copies are still available." Because of the publication of this
paragraph, a very hard-working and useful member of the staff
resigned from the committee of the school newspaper.

The newspaper was partially financed by a large number of
advertisements. Since parents read the paper, local traders felt that
this was a good medium for advertising. To illustrate these advertisements, pupils in the art rooms made the drawings of cycles, ice cream
cones, vacuum cleaners, shoes, fish, fruit, paint brushes and rollers,
radios, hair styles, books, and a grocer's weighing machine. Pupils in
the commercial department looked after the sending out of accounts
and reminding advertisers to renew their contracts.

The newspaper failed and closed down. The failure was partly due to the discouragement of many teachers who were unenthusiastic when pupils wanted help and advice in writing articles, selling advertising space and selling copies of the paper. There was a feeling that this wasn't real education; this wasn't the purpose for which the school was built. This was part and parcel of the erosion of standards, of pupils' lib, juvenile delinquency, truancy, escape from hard work, retreat from Scotland's educational tradition. But a simpler explanation is possible; maybe the newspaper wasn't interesting enough to have a mass appeal for pupils.

When I arrived at Summerhill I had not fully realised the difficulties and dangers of democracy. My predecessor had, in a kind and generous and enlightened manner, laid down the law. I wanted to widen the area of staff and pupil participation. I hadn't sufficiently realised how far from democracy Britain lingered, or the nature of the pressures that gently or forcibly pushed central and local government into the hands of a few people, kidding the rest that they were playing the major part in the vital decisions. The problems we met in Summerhill in trying to establish a school democracy were largely the same problems that prevented the House of Commons from being a democratic convention.

The staff also found it difficult to work out methods of expressing their joint opinions and putting them into effect. As the school grew, various staff committees were formed. There was a Standing Committee whose function was the subject of frequent debate, never satisfactorily finalised. The intention was that, besides administering and disbursing the school fund, it would make decisions on questions demanding immediate answers for which the calling of a staff meeting would be too slow and cumbersome a process. It was agreed that the Standing Committee would refer major decisions to the staff meeting, and it was assumed that on other questions the staff meeting would support the Standing Committee's decisions. Difficulty arose when some members of the staff sought to overrule a Standing Committee decision on a minor topic.

There were a Cottage Committee, which administered the school's cottage 20 miles west of Aberdeen in the Dee Valley, a Social Committee, a Tea Committee, regular meetings in separate groups of heads of departments, year masters, senior staff (headmaster, deputy heads and assistant heads) and the staff meeting.

Heads of departments (principal teachers) and year masters were paid on the same scales. Some of the heads of departments viewed the new institution of year masters with suspicion. Several of the year masters and mistresses were younger, the job seemed to be less burdened with laborious detail, and some of the form teachers and assistant teachers felt that the year masters were being paid extra rates for a job that the assistant teachers had usually regarded as part of their function, the welfare of pupils. Aberdeen gave each of its comprehensive schools freedom to describe the function of the year staff in its own way.

At the first meeting of the year masters and year mistresses I suggested that, for some of our pupils, life was harsher and colder than at any time since Oliver Twist. They returned after school to an empty house, both parents were working and had little leisure or patience to listen to their stories on an evening. The Church played a part in few of their lives. The doctors had queues outside their surgeries and hadn't enough time to talk to parents and discuss the upbringing of children. There was a new need for guidance and help. For some pupils a sympathetic year master or mistress was the only adult in the wide world they could turn to for help. As I saw it, the year master was the counsel for the defence. There might be private occasions when the counsel for the defence told off his client, giving him sturdy advice but in public the year master must be on the pupils' side and must be seen to be on the pupils' side. If the pupils trusted them they would be a success. It was not their job to deal out punishment any more than it was the job of a defence counsel to deal out punishment. These new appointments were part of a salvage operation. Suddenly Scottish education was wakening up from its long sleep. The child was being put in the centre of the scene. I read later in a book of Lyward's, "The key to all deeper insight into human behaviour is not technical proficiency but simply love." From this source a new ray of comprehension expanded into the classroom, initiating a great change in human relationships within the educational provision.

In the midst of all these democratic processes, many of the older members of the staff longed for the simpler days of my more autocratic predecessor; and, at the time, accused me of being dictatorial since I had refused to take a staff vote on whether we should revert to a wide-scale use of corporal punishment. I knew that if I took a vote, I'd lose. There was a restlessness but also an invigoration in this clash between two totally different interpretations of how to bring up the young. Under continual discussion and enquiry, fixed ideas were dissolving. Or like icebergs breaking up, pieces detaching themselves, grinding together, a commotion of ideas. Everything was under inspection. Not only what democracy was and how it could be made to work, but also its implications. For example, what's the democratic way to select staff? The democratic processes are more fallible, human and humorous than they appear in the textbooks. In St Nicholas House a subcommittee interviewed applicants for a post as year mistress. One of them was a charming Ulster girl, religious, a loyal Protestant. "She spoke like Bernadette Devlin," said one of the committee, eliminating her from his list.

As soon as a technical question was asked, or any question to which the candidates gave a detailed answer outwith the experience of the committee members, a glazed look came into their eyes. Candidates for the job of English teacher were asked if they thought an English teacher should be concerned primarily with helping pupils to acquire linguistic skills or handing on the literary traditions of Scotland, or something else. It could be regarded as a good question. The candidates took the question seriously and answered it at length. When the interviews were over the committee sighed and said what long-winded fellows these English teachers are. As soon as their words ceased to be of the nature of slogans or headlines, the committee lost interest. I don't blame them for losing interest. If I were a lay member of a committee appointing a medical officer of health I would quickly get bored at a discussion on the fluoridation of water. Much more work should be done enquiring into how we improve on these selection processes. It's a human problem, and human ingenuity can solve it. We are an underdeveloped nation as far as our ability to cope with the details of public life and government are concerned. The current type of selection interview allocates success to the crafty candidate who has sized up the interviewing panel and knows how to handle them, throwing in a joke here and an appeal to emotion there, and above all, entertaining them and remembering that they get their coffee at 11 and that with every word he speaks thereafter their coffee is getting colder. But none of this is new. Shakespeare observed it. He said that people like "gawds" (gaudy things),

And give to dust that is a little gilt
More laud than gold o'er-dusted.

More frequently the councillors genuinely try to assess the candidates, doing everything they can to make an appointment in the best interests of the pupils, but the information available to them is limited and liable to error. The director of education has sought a report from the directors of the areas where the candidates have been teaching and the headmaster has consulted the headmasters. I sometimes found that a headmaster I consulted was telling me more about himself than about the candidate. "This man has some way-out ideas on education" could mean that the candidate was not a good teacher; but it might mean that the headmaster was a martinet. "This woman is loyal and co-operative" might mean that she made his coffee and never contradicted him. Scottish headmasters are more limited than their English colleagues in describing a teacher. The Scots would say, "This man has an excellent record of Highers passes and he is a good disciplinarian. He is nevertheless respected by his pupils. He is popular with his colleagues. He gives up his free

time generously in extra-mural activities. He has attended several
in-service courses." That is the stereotype. English headmasters
would give a fuller, more relaxed account of an applicant. They would
throw in details which in Scotland might be considered frivolous and
irrelevant. What does it matter, a Scottish dominie might say, that a
history teacher keeps hens or grows his own vegetables or has
translated Dante or paints or is a glider pilot? In Scotland the
teacher's aim is usually limited to putting across information about
history and a good history technician will meet the requirements. But
I was trying to find teachers who were more than good instructors in
their speciality and were able to communicate easily with children
and teach history in a way that helped them to understand more about
living. The English assessments were more useful for this purpose.

One appointment had a particular effect on the school. The deputy
director of education had gone through the list of applicants for the
post of deputy head of the school and agreed on a short leet. The
Education Committee added another name to the leet. Only three
councillors turned up to interview candidates. After the interview the
three councillors selected the candidate whom they had added to the
leet. He had less experience than the others and he was a supporter of
corporal punishment. He had previously been a Labour member of
the town council. His appointment fortified the teachers who believed
in corporal punishment and was a turning-point in the campaign. The
local Labour Party was deeply divided over this issue and a senior
office-bearer threatened to resign, but the minority had finally to
support the majority. A local M.P. told me that in the interests of the
school I should accept the appointment with good grace.

I think the best way we can hope to ensure democracy in Scotland is
to tell the pupils how immature an institution it still is. We should tell
them the full story of how it works, the humour, the dirty deals, the
pressures, the selfless work. They are attracted by a true story. They
lose interest in a formal drama in which the characters are as remote
from real life as Aberdeen's toga-ed statues. We want to bring reality
into education.

I think the old traditional Scottish readiness to be fobbed off with a
fine windy generalisation is ebbing. When the candidates for the
English vacancy in Summerhill were asked if an English teacher
should be concerned primarily to hand on the Scottish literary
tradition, I wondered just what the interviewing panel thought the
Scottish literary tradition really was. When I was at school it meant
memorising Burns's mouse and daisy, reciting **To a Haggis** at a
Burns supper, writing a Highers answer about Meg Merrilies or
Bailie Nicol Jarvie or the Little Minister. Later MacDiarmid and
Lewis Grassic Gibbon were let in on condition that they didn't
mention communism. All that's changing. We're enquiring more
closely into these things.

At the end of the Edinburgh Festival a Scottish historian, Julia Buckroyd, discussed in a **Scotsman** article how little nourishment Scotland has drawn from its traditions and history to give to its people. Scotland's past was regarded as quaint. "The mythology and romanticism as commonly understood has deprived ordinary people of a sense of history and continuity. . . . (There is) mawkish nostalgia for a Scottish society which never existed and is infinitely removed from the reality of the industrial Lowlands where most Scots live. . . . Most Scots live in an uneasy limbo between the past and the future, neither knowing how they have emerged into the present, nor what the future can hold. If, as seems possible, some degree of independence is conceded to Scotland within the foreseeable future, then the fate of the country will lie in the hands of Scots themselves."

Many Scottish education committee members, interviewing teachers and subscribing to the current mythology of "the Scottish literary tradition", haven't themselves had the kind of education which would help them to discriminate between the mythology and the reality. Thus they perpetuate the mythology in their schools and will make it more difficult for young Scots to act with understanding when they take the fate of the country into their own hands.

The Scottish churches hang on tenaciously to their temporal power (for example, ministers on education committees help to appoint teachers acceptable to them) and in this way wield an undemocratic influence out of proportion to the size of their dwindling congregations. Aberdeen Education Committee decided to upgrade the study of religious education in all its comprehensive schools by appointing to each a specialist teacher in charge of religious education. In my opinion the best of the applicants for this appointment was a laicised Roman Catholic priest of 28, an Oxford graduate, who had had a row with his bishop over the role of the priesthood in modern industrial society. As a Jesuit priest he had worked together with Marxists in London and Paris. But the ministers of the Church of Scotland were having no truck with any kind of Catholic on the ground, I was told, that since no Catholic school would appoint a Protestant to be in charge of its religious education, therefore no Protestant school would admit a Catholic to be in charge of **its** religious education. Besides, they added, the fact that he had been laicised was hardly an argument in his favour. These arguments are hard to follow. I am not a Christian, but I was happy to have found an applicant who would present living Christian values to our pupils and help them to face the deep and dangerous issues of life. He was concerned to help them, not to indoctrinate them. The ministers would have said how could we be sure of that? All I could answer was that I felt I could trust him. I was hoping to recruit at Summerhill a staff who, whatever their individual labels might be, would have in common a desire to help all pupils equally. That is the climate in which discussion, however vigorous, is a liberating experience. The future of democracy depends on this vital communication and fruitful exchange of ideas among people who are more than their labels, people whom we trust so much that when we are arguing with them we feel not combative, resistant to an indoctrinator, but that we are sharing in the search for truth.

Almost always there was this fundamentally conservative resistance to ideas which involved trust (and therefore risk) and change. They were playing safe. When I pleaded for changes in school usages, the administrators and education committee members said, "You must wait until you have persuaded the majority to accept your point of view," knowing that the tools of effective counter-persuasion are in their hands. If we had small school communities our discussions would be more nourishing. But the indoctrinators fear such relaxed, enquiring communication. That is why they favour the great increase in size of schools (and regions of government).

Summerhill is too big for one school. The arguments in favour of a big school are few, and these largely deal with what is convenient for the administrators. A dozen years ago, when Summerhill opened, both of the main political parties declared themselves to be against big schools. The big schools have crept in when nobody was looking. It was a tune called by the administrators in defiance of the Members of Parliament. There was a distinguished report on secondary education, published in 1947 by the Advisory Council on Education in Scotland and written by Sir James Robertson (who later performed the opening ceremony when Summerhill began as a junior secondary school). It stated: "We have reached the conclusion that the maximum secondary roll should be 600. . . . It follows that we cannot recommend the setting up of huge multilateral schools on the American model, as favoured by the London County Council, with 2,000 or more pupils in each. The unity we seek is organic, not merely administrative, and we do not believe it can be realised with such vast numbers merely by setting a collection of sub-schools of different kinds on a common campus and calling them one school. In this connection the university or institute, with constituent colleges, affords no safe analogy for the school life of children and adolescents."

Having worked in a Fife school of 500 pupils and then in Summerhill which had over 1,000 pupils, I was aware of what Robertson's committee meant by organic unit, and of the serious disadvantages of big schools. Even in minor routine matters the big school is crippled by disadvantages unknown to smaller schools. A disproportionate amount of time has to be spent in regulating traffic to avoid overcrowding at peak periods. A disproportionate amount of time is taken by pupils walking long distances from one classroom to another. Lockers are not used if pupils have to make a long journey back to them; thus the pupils carry their belongings around with them. During his secondary career in a school of 1,000 a pupil is likely to be taught by twice as many teachers as in a school of 500, and he is likely to be taught in twice as many rooms. Teachers are ships that pass in the night, briefly communicating and then disappearing; a classroom is an impersonal roll-call room with desks, not a known haven. Some local authorities, such as Aberdeen, decided not to build any more school assembly halls since a hall to contain the whole school is prohibitively expensive. That means that the school can never meet comfortably as a corporate group, and a sense of identity, of belonging, is lost. A small school has none of these disadvantages.

One advantage, often overlooked, of having a small school is that there is a small staff. At Summerhill there was staff of nearly 100 and a staff meeting was a public meeting at which a few teachers, practised in public speaking, spoke frequently, and the great majority rarely contributed. The meeting was a public contest in scoring debating points. Several meetings had a cup-tie suspense brooding over them. There was a ruthlessness, an uncompromising spirit, in which to admit a mistake or accept a modification was regarded as a score to the other side, and the meeting was a spectacle for the winning of the support of those in the middle. It was as likely to provide educational wisdom in a heckling meeting, as a general election is to provide political wisdom. The wisecrack, the smart answer, the apparently incontrovertible citing of statistics and a knowledge of procedure were the weapons by which opinions were swayed and decisions won. Politically we haven't moved all that far from Mr Pickwick's experience of the hustings of Eatanswill. Ordinary human wisdom and experience and understanding, being undervalued, doesn't come enough into the reckoning. It is only when we have a small staff that we get away from the procedures and the scoring of points to something like a family situation where people can admit mistakes and incorporate criticism into a modified policy without loss of face.

A large part of the staff meetings were spent in discussing the daily mechanics of running a school. We discussed how to spend the staff tuckshop profit, homework, parents' meetings, the maintenance and running costs of the three buses owned by the school, parking, the collection of dinner money, raising money for the school fund by the organising of a fair, school visits, pupils wandering in corridors, informing parents who received the family income supplement that their children were eligible for free meals, fire drills, liaison with industry, staff entertainments, organising a careers convention, school reports. There was rarely any difficulty over these things and almost all members of the staff were ready to co-operate and help and shoulder extra burdens to help the school to run efficiently.

Trouble arose when I prefaced a meeting with a short talk (five to seven minutes) on some subject of wider interest. I wanted to spend a part of the staff meeting linking the school's work to wider issues, to encourage the staff (and particularly the younger teachers) to think not only on **how** but also **why**. For example, I reported on a conference on drugs which I had attended. Ninety per cent of the population of a housing estate (we were told) took drugs once a month; if a child was over 16, parents couldn't be informed of the child's drug-taking without the child's consent; there were 18 narcotic addicts at that time registered in Aberdeen. Another subject was the differences made by the Social Work Act of 1968. On another occasion I summarised a talk given by Professor Dennis Gabor, Nobel prize-winner in physics, who said that our present material wealth would run out and that, unless there was new thinking in science, human history would consist of a few centuries of wealth on either side of which were hundreds of thousands of years of darkness; and I suggested that we teachers should be now engaged in the fundamental rethinking in education that this assumption implied.

Major opposition was raised when I gave a short talk on school policy. Up till then there had been an uneasy compromise. The talk defined attitudes and I outline it here in some detail.

In the old days (I said) education was largely the job of transmitting information, and differing attitudes of teachers were less important. Today, when we were shouldered with responsibility for wider burdens, it was more important that we should have a consistent attitude towards pupils. In an authoritarian school the pupils knew where they were. In a progressive school, the pupils knew where they were. But in a school which had teachers in both camps, the pupils were confused. In the future this question of consistency of attitude would keep on arising. It didn't mean having a school where everybody agreed about everything, but it did mean broad agreement on attitudes to pupils and especially on attitudes to punishment. In changing times we had to reassess the role of the teacher and there was no outside authority which knew more about it than we did; for the answers to the new questions thrown at us we had nobody to rely on but ourselves. For this purpose it was advisable to encourage young teachers to be much more involved in the working out of policy, the carrying out of experiment, the enquiry into new ideas and new kinds of curricula. We had to make use of this initiative, these insights, sympathies and energies, the more so since the younger teachers were nearer to the pupils.

There were two areas which especially required new initiatives. For one session the staff had followed and discussed the television programmes about coping with the problems set by the raising of the school-leaving age, but these programmes were, on the whole, so dull and unhelpful that the staff voted not to follow the television series during the following session. That meant working out better curricula for ourselves. It was a good area for experiment, unhampered by examinations. Would the pupils, for example, be interested in intensively learning a language? A Nuffield enquiry had shown that after 70 hours of learning a language (35 hours a week for two weeks), students had passed the "O" level in that language. Normally 750 hours had been required if pupils were to reach that level. We could enquire into what was possible at Summerhill. We could make a different kind of timetable altogether; for example a group might want to use a month to produce a play.

We should enquire also into the best way to educate those pupils who had become delinquent. At the Aberdeen conference on drugs a speaker said that "a society can control only those who value their membership in it". How did we create in the school a society of which the delinquent pupils and those on the edge of delinquency would value membership?

We wanted teachers who would evolve ideas and try to put them into practice. If there were members of the staff who did not feel they could work happily in this more experimental, more permissive climate, they should feel free to ask for a transfer. I wanted volunteers prepared to re-examine attitudes and accepted opinions and present a blueprint for a new educational outlook.

Chapter Six

CONFRONTATION

It was the statement about feeling free to apply for a transfer that several of the more traditionalist members of the staff objected to. It precipitated the showdown. With hindsight I think the crisis could have been avoided but only at the cost of greater compromise and a further uneasy period of wary administration like the tenancy of a government unsupported by a good majority. Long ago one of my teachers used to tell us, "The man who aims at nothing in particular generally hits his mark." I think this is what has happened to government and schools in Britain. The diplomats and fixers run the show, fortified by comforting words and phrases like statesmanship and the doctrine of the mean, and are so busy finding a formula and maintaining equilibrium that they have no time left to give to their business of recreating a living democracy or a nourishing system of education. I think that this pressure on politicians and teachers to train in maintaining an equilibrium is part of the establishment's strategy to defend itself; if you get a senior job you're so busy maintaining your balance and not falling off that you don't get involved in major changes; maintaining the balance is merely maintaining the status quo. The balancing gives the illusion of movement, but you are staying in the same place. I think we're coming to the end of this undistinguished phase of our political and educational history. A more resolute younger generation may sweep away this highly convoluted ritual and its accompanying inertia, and initiate a simpler programme of political and educational change. Several of the middle of the road heads of departments said I had "polarised" the staff. But I don't think there is any future in this strategy of covering over differences of opinion and pretending that they are not vital. This is the task that politicians and teachers have to deal with — how do you run a school or run a country without pretending that vital differences of opinion don't exist?

About a month after I made the policy declaration, half of the staff signed a document drawing the director of education's attention to the policy declaration and their concern about the school. They said that many teachers, many parents, even many pupils, many institutions and other agencies, local and outwith the district, felt that the policies of the school were likely to achieve "the continual and rapidly deteriorating situation presently existing in many areas of the school's functioning". They felt that the root of the problem lay in the question of authority and claimed "that so-called anti-authoritarianism is fashionable and that the collapse of secular and learned authority in our society has inevitably affected our schools. . . . It is the basic premise of this document that authority must exist because it is necessary for the maintenance of any form of pluralistic society, and that this is particularly relevant to the specialised society of a school". There followed a report of the type of incidents which had caused consternation to half of the staff.

Their statement listed apathy to work, recalcitrance, dress, manners, obscenities, vandalism, violence, intimidation, extortion, theft, truancy, dangerous behaviour, the number of pupils who didn't accept reprimand. Two subjects on the list deserve further mention. One was speech. "Few pupils now even attempt any form of acceptable speech," said the statement. I remembered a professor of Rhodes University College in South Africa, a graduate of Aberdeen, who told me that his white students said "sir" to him but that his black students at a different college didn't. Now our Summerhill pupils were at the same stage of transition. They felt, like the black South African students, that the use of "sir" was an acceptance of deference, a sign of submission, which the harder, bolder spirits were not prepared to give. There are other evidences of the pressures upon groups at a stage of transition. A group is suspicious of those of its members who are extra polite to those who are seen to be on a different social plane; "sucking up" is the phrase used to describe this attitude. Trade unionists suspect workmen who are sucking up to the boss. Black students suspect those who are sucking up to the white professor. Servicemen suspect those who are sucking up to the officers; a too-smart salute, a too-ready politeness are regarded as a sign that so-and-so is sweating on his commission. Similarly, pupils are escaping from the attitudes and forms of deference, the salute, the "sir", the acceptance without argument of the teacher's **ipse dixit**. This is where the fundamental cleavage in the Summerhill staff lay. Half of the staff saw these expressions of pupil opinion as a disaster. When obedience and deference decreased, they foresaw the end of society as they had known it. A Fife contractor advised his fellow employers on how to deal with their Irish labourers. "When they stop saying 'sir', sack them."

But there was another reason for the form of the pupils' speech that these teachers found unacceptable. The speech that was insisted on in the classroom was different from the speech in the pupils' homes. In no part of Scotland has the traditional Scottish speech survived so strongly as in Aberdeenshire and the north-east. Some pupils find little difficulty in being bi-lingual; others are obviously translating the home speech into the standard Scottish-English insisted on in most schools. Humorous stories are told about literal translations of Scottish idioms. In Aberdeenshire, enquiring about our neighbour's health we ask "Fit like are ye the day?" Well-brought-up people translate this literally into "What like are you today?" unaware that the idiom is not standard English. Some of the more independent-minded Aberdonians, and especially younger Aberdonians, make fun of this unsuccessful effort at translation.

People may say, "In a book about education, what's the relevance of all this about local speech?" I think it is central to the Summerhill story, which is the story of pupils who refuse to be steamrollered into an acceptable middle-class, London-dictated mould. It is one of the facets in the story of a society in transition. Political and educational overtones are rarely absent from this theme of speech patterns.

If the Summerhill pupils spoke in the historic accents of their homes, it was regarded as outlandish and uncouth and impolite. If they modified their speech too much to the required English pattern, they were regarded as letting their own side down. Sometimes when I asked them a question they would give the answer "aye", which was immediately translated into what teachers regard as the "proper" word, "yes". A growing number of working-class children in Aberdeen see standard English as the imposed, required speech, the use of which, like the use of "sir", will be a sign that they accept the rules and regulations, the deference due and the obedience expected. It is a sign of submission to the imposed culture. I was brought up in this attitude of deference to the required speech. The local words were "vulgar", not as bad as swearing but nevertheless to be avoided by all well-brought-up children. You could play tennis for a whole, long, summer afternoon and evening at our village tennis club and never hear this standard Scottish-English departed from. Later, studying German, I was surprised to find that many German words were pronounced in the Scottish way (for example, **finger**), and it was strange to find this pronunciation, not respectable in Scotland, regarded as respectable and acceptable in Germany. It was like finding a local farmworker at a seat of honour at an embassy banquet. I felt like asking, "How did you get in here?" Thus the teachers who didn't find the speech of many of their pupils acceptable were unaware alike of the long history of the local speech and of the pressures brought upon young people by the collision of two cultures.

The second subject on the list of things found unacceptable to the traditionalist teachers was "manners and courtesy". They declared that "the simplest courtesies have virtually disappeared". I don't know what "virtually" means and I suspect that it is a rhetorical word which suggests more than it is prepared to say. Few pupils were discourteous to teachers whom they liked, or whom they disliked but respected for their fairness. Occasionally after a school lunch a year mistress invited me to her room for coffee. Boys and girls of her year relaxed on chairs or sitting on the floor. They discussed many things. After she had expressed an opinion, a pupil might say, "I think that's daft, Betsy." Is that discourtesy? I don't think so. This situation merits a closer enquiry, because a period of transition is composed of countless millions of individual confrontations. These young Scotsmen and Scotswomen, clamouring for emancipation from the attitudes of deference that had affected them from birth, found themselves in a new, free and slightly unnerving situation in which a senior member of the staff treated them as equals, was obviously fond of them and concerned for their welfare, was prepared to listen to their opinions. The pupils' first reaction was that this was phoney; they had met it before. And then they found that it wasn't phoney; it was real. Here was a year mistress who made no pretensions to superior wisdom, who was prepared to discuss their problems, including their sex problems, without asserting that she possessed the final wisdom, who was delighted that they should call her by her first name. A new planet had swum into their ken and they were at first nonplussed. They wanted to try how far she would allow them to go. Will she think this question is cheek and bawl me out for asking it? In these exchanges I sensed the tremulous efforts of uncertain young people to find their footing. She had one of the most difficult year groups to cope with˚ and sometimes found them trying and occasionally unendurable. I thought of Paul writing to the people of Corinth to tell them that love "beareth all things, believeth all things, hopeth all things, endureth all things"; of Christ telling the people of Galilee to forgive unto seventy times seven. I compared Betsy with some of the other teachers who insisted on the outward forms of respect. One of them said, "I don't care what the pupils feel towards me as long as they show me the forms of respect." Betsy was different. I don't think the word "respect" played much part in her vocabulary; she didn't ask for the outward forms and I don't think she was all that concerned about whether they felt respect for her. It's comforting to feel that the pupils do respect you, but a yearning for either the outward forms or the inner reality may be an admission of inadequacy and of the need for reassurance.

The staff document listed the demoralising effect that pupils were having on some members of the staff, claiming that the teachers were losing heart, turning a blind eye on misdemeanours, feeling that their status was being lowered. One sentence said, "They object to their professionality being questioned and unrecognised," and the list of their charges against me said I supported the pupil against the teacher, appeared to be "interested only in the recalcitrant", discouraged the use of sanctions, and "denied the professionality of teacher who refuse to accept offensive insults from pupils". Another charge said, "The head teacher frequently used the captive audience of the school assembly for disseminating his personal views, which are often at variance with the consciences of many who are required to listen to them and which, in some opinions, appear to go far beyond his remit either as a teacher or head teacher."

I had frequently offered to them, or to any member of the staff, the opportunity to take the morning assembly and make a statement of any religious or educational or political beliefs they held. I had hoped they would seize the opportunity and present to the pupils varying views of our life and society so that the pupils should be aware how much adults differ in their opinions. That, I thought, would be preferable to the usual effort to try and offer an objective view. But in six years not one member of the staff took up the offer.

For years I had been trying to bring life back into the morning assembly. In most schools it is a lifeless ritual. Usually it consists of a hymn, a prayer, a reading, and then the announcements. Few of the pupils sing the hymn or listen to the prayer. I think there is value in an assembly; pupils become aware of themselves as members of a community, and a regular gathering like this can help pupils to understand what the school as a community is trying to do, and the pupils have an opportunity to learn what other parts of their own community have been doing. I tried to show how our community was related to other communities such as the town council, Parliament, local schools for handicapped pupils, mental hospitals, social service workers. I think it is a mistake to pretend to objectivity in these talks. What generally happens is that in the assembly as in (for example) the history books, the establishment point of view is put across as if it were the sensible point of view and any deviations from it regarded as subjective and prejudiced. I tried to speak simply and in concrete terms. Describing the carnage in the First World War I said that our school hall held 1,000 people and indicated what area of Aberdeen would be included if the pupils imagined all the casualties to be in groups of a thousand in halls the size of ours, built close together. I spoke of the life of old people, hoping against hope to be remembered by their relations who were usually so busy with their own affairs that they remembered them only on their birthdays. On the morning after the pipes and drums of the Gordon Highlanders had produced a concert in the school, I pointed out to the pupils that, excellent although the concert had been, they shouldn't be taken in by the music, the tartan, the advertisements about the opportunities for sport and seeing the world that the army produced. This was the point where the traditionalist teachers became angry. They said that the pupils in the morning assembly were a captive audience and I shouldn't discourage army recruiting. A Liberal member of

Aberdeen Town Council proposed that the armed services shouldn't be allowed to enter Aberdeen schools for the purposes of recruiting, but the majority Labour Party in Aberdeen overruled him.

Summerhill was a test case in which the Labour Party, on the retreat from the issues with which it had been identified since the time of Keir Hardie, was being pressed by a small right-wing group of teachers. Labour was less inclined to fight for these issues, becoming more like Tories. Labour believed in corporal punishment, the fighting services, the traditionalist education system and its authoritarian foundation. The erosion of Labour principles is inseparable from the floating of Labour M.P.s and trade union leaders into commanding positions in our society such as head of the Coal Board and railways. The general secretary of the National Union of Railwaymen became a governor of the Bank of England and a director of the Rio Tinto Zinc Company, and got a seat in the House of Lords. Summerhill was a minor incident in the Labour erosion, a position they were prepared to yield. The Labour Lord Provost of Aberdeen, whose father had fought a battle against corporal punishment and who himself described the belting of pupils as "an obscenity", was not prepared to take up the fight. He is now in the House of Lords. An Aberdeen Labour M.P., who was on the record as being opposed to corporal punishment and who was the Minister in charge of Scottish education when the issue was being fought out at Summerhill, didn't raise his voice. And this at a time when a historian or a foreigner, reading the latest Acts of Parliament, would have assumed that the laws dealing with children were becoming less punitive. The "Kilbrandon Act" had put a new emphasis on healing and much less emphasis on punishment. In these apparently easier circumstances, why didn't the Lord Provost and the Minister proclaim when in power the things they had believed in when in opposition? The Labour councillors mostly responsible for my appointment to Summerhill had something of the outlook of Keir Hardie. Their successors had become more like Harold Wilson.

The convener of the Education Committee sought to do justice between the many clamant voices besieging his ear to the traditionalist teachers and their unions; the teachers who wanted to abolish corporal punishment; the divided parents; the kirks; the writers of letters to the newspapers. He was a straightforward man but tossed about hopelessly in a revolutionary turmoil, clutching at straws, buffetted by newspaper headlines. He believed the teachers in conference could settle their differences and reach what he called a "consensus", and to this end he divided them up into small groups and set times for regular discussions that lasted several weeks. They were to work out "a draft code of principles of conduct for pupils" But the minority of the staff who supported new initiatives felt that the wording of this remit failed to do justice to the case they were presenting. The convener and the Education Committee were begging the question. The staff minority didn't believe that the difficulties could be settled by the imposition of a new code of rules. That was the main division underlying the weeks of discussion that followed. All of the small groups set up by the convener met weekly. There were also meetings of other small groups and large groups, hastily announced meetings, long-prepared meetings, secret meetings, meetings of the Education Committee representatives with delegates of different staff groups. When the officially appointed staff groups completed their discussions, each group summarised its findings, and the chairman of the groups met a senior administrator to aggregate the summaries and turn them into the consensus hoped for by the convener.

The resulting Summerhill document on school rules was a mixture of unanimous agreement on non-controversial subjects (for example, on fire precautions) and majority votes on controversial subjects. The idea that this was a consensus was later dropped, but the attempt illustrated how a word can be recruited into a campaign to influence public opinion by blurring the real dividing issues (in this case making the parents believe that the teachers had sunk their differences). The remit to the teachers had been to agree on a code of principles of conduct for pupils and to suggest how "aberrations" should be dealt with. The first sentence of the document described its contents. "It is our aim to establish a healthy climate in which learning and teaching can most effectively take place within the school community." When the majority said "learning and teaching" they meant the traditional work that goes on in Scottish secondary schools, the usual examination-based subjects. They saw education as the putting of information into children's heads, and they saw their remit as how to establish quietness in the classroom so that this transfer of information could proceed without unseemly interruption. "Pray silence for the textbooks, and the teachers who convey their message to us." But a large minority of us were not interested in methods of keeping pupils quiet and receptive while all this information was being given to them; we were questioning the whole transaction, and denying that it was education. Two teachers wrote that this document, produced after 800 working hours, enshrined the attitudes of the vast majority of "moderate teachers". "Beneath the gloss of progressive vocabulary, videotape recorders, carpeted sixth form   social areas and the like, perhaps the attitudes of teachers remain distressingly unchanged." The majority were "people who have assimilated all the progressive educational jargon but who, in practice, fall back on methods which are primitive and rights which appear to derive from the feudal overlord" and they concluded that "there is very little warmth and humanity in the document".

The document has a historical interest as a statement of how a

majority of teachers in a Scottish secondary school in the 1970s
viewed their function. In a list of **Rules for Pupils**, it said: "Do not act
in a way likely to bring disrepute to yourself, to your parents or to the
school", and it gave instances of the actions it had in mind — "lying,
stealing, swearing, persistent bad conduct, disruptive or improper
behaviour, offensive behaviour — e.g. acts of violence, bullying,
intimidation, extortion, truancy, vandalism, smoking, consumption
of alcohol and misuse of drugs". I too had committed most of these
sins but, being an adult, wouldn't be punished. Punishment was
confined to children.

That sentence was reminiscent of an Aberdeen educational
document of 300 years earlier. In his **History of the Scottish People**,
Professor Smout writes: "In 1675 the Synod of Aberdeen asked its
presbyteries only to demand three questions of the schoolmaster:
whether he makes the bairns learn the catechism, whether he teaches
them prayers for morning and evening and a grace for meals and
whether 'he chastises them for cursing, swearing, lying, speaking
profanietie; for disobedience to parents and what vices that appeares
in them'."

The tradition of sin and punishment is deep in Scottish education.
The Summerhill document emphasised how difficult it is for us
Scottish teachers to escape from our Calvinist inheritance. The
rebuke of a 17th century minister of the kirk could be heard in these
sentences from the 20th century document — "All teachers have a
crucial part to play in implementing the rules and in setting an
example. Opting out, ignoring situations and relying on arbitrary
sanctions are to be deplored."

This seems to apply to those teachers who see some offence being
committed and look the other way; and those who give six of the belt
when the code lays down two. But it was also hitting against the year
master who, knowing the home background of an offender, decided to
forgive him; that was opting out. Not only did the authoritarians want
to punish; they resented other teachers who didn't punish. They felt
uneasy when these other teachers established friendly relationships
with the pupils, and if a year master or mistress (as had happened)
told a pupil that he had offended against society and that he should
make it up to society (should atone to society, which really means
becoming reunited to society, **at one** with society) by working for two
days of his Christmas holidays in a mental hospital or school for
handicapped children, that would be prohibited as being an
"arbitrary sanction", not included in the sanctions "recognised and
accepted by all'.

(There was a humorous situation one Christmas when a sinner,
asked to give up two days for this purpose, had expressed such delight
at finding something interesting to do during what might otherwise
have been a dull fortnight, that the voice of my Calvinist education

whispered to me that something had gone wrong. Deep down, I, too, wanted her to be punished. I felt that expiation contained a sense of retribution, but if the girl was so obviously going to enjoy helping old people at Christmas, we had missed out on her reformation. I mention the incident to show how completely the two outlooks on life are divided.)

One paragraph of the staff majority document said that, "It is necessary to have a framework of community living which is recognised and accepted by all." It sounded innocent and reasonable. But what it was really saying was that there was no place in the school for those whose outlook on life was fundamentally different from this regimen of rules and sanctions. This is the situation in Russia, where sanctions have been used against writers who questioned the "framework of community living". Until our own time the school has been an authoritarian place because the pupils didn't dare challenge its authority. Now fitter, better fed, more enquiring, pupils are challenging the school's authority. There are two different ways of meeting this challenge. One is to alter the curriculum and to give pupils help and understanding. The other way, advocated in the **Black Papers**, is to reassert the authoritarian control and reinforce the sanctions. Once again the controversy in the school was a microcosm of the controversy throughout the world. Do we impose order and crush the exasperating dissidents? Or do we undertake the much harder job of creating a society capable of containing in harmony people of widely varying outlook? Such a society would reconsider the whole conception of law.

Equally dangerous was the statement in the document that disruptive and disturbed pupils were to be readily identified. It seemed to suggest that teachers would know who the disturbed children were, so that they would be patient with them; but experience of Summerhill showed that, once these pupils had been identified, some teachers took it out of them. And not only out of the pupils, but out of their brothers and sisters. We had a former pupil who gave much trouble to the school and much unhappiness to his parents, whom I'd met several times. A younger son, on arrival from the primary school, was stigmatised in front of his classmates as the brother of ———. He rushed home sobbing, and his father came to see me, very disturbed, asking if his brother's sins were to be visited on the young boy and if he were to go through Summerhill known to all the teachers as the brother of ———. The mother was again attending the doctor as a result of this upset. But the Education Committee insisted that Summerhill should accept also this new rule that all disruptive and disturbed children were to be readily identifiable.

Another rule insisted on by the Education Committee asserted the right of any teacher without consultation to contact the police. Previously the police had been called in only as a last resort. And there were to be regular staff meetings "to check on implementation of rules". It was not only the pupils who were to be checked up on; it was also the teachers. Once you make rules for teachers (as well as pupils) you have to set up the machinery for ensuring that they are followed. That means collecting and sifting information and presenting it at a court educational (like a court martial). That is how the Covenanters imposed their rules of righteousness on backsliding sinners.

Another recommendation stated: "It is desirable that we win the support of the pupils for the rules. These rules should be discussed at the School Council. As well as receiving copies of the rules, pupils should be given time to discuss these at form and year meetings. In addition, every opportunity should be taken to emphasise that head teacher and staff agree with these rules and expect them to be observed." The document was saying to pupils, "Here are the rules. Discuss them. But remember that we expect you to obey them." The School Council was put in its place as part of the machinery for propagating the acceptable principles on which the school rules were based. In a similar way a colonial power tells a native council how it is expected to operate. I took this up with the administrator who was overseeing the exercise and asked him what kind of discussion the School Council could have about rules thus imposed on them. He replied, "Well, the council may make proposals for modifying the rules." I imagined the answer the pupils of the council might make to that invitation — "Big deal!"

The minority group of teachers drew up their own report. They pointed out that it was not a simple matter to make a code of discipline for a community because communities vary greatly (the prison, the village, the factory, the family, the school) and have different goals. A list of specific rules of conduct was closer to the practice of the prison and factory than the neighbourhood and family. Many children find it hard to acquiesce in these school rules "because the children's values do not coincide with the values of the school; because the goals of the examination obstacle race are unobtainable by them and its processes considered irrelevant or difficult". They said that the school rules of the staff majority implied that we could solve problems of behaviour within a school, irrespective of what was happening outside the school. But there were conflicts of standards, conflicts of loyalties, and the pupil was influenced by other things outside the school — "the organised and official vandalism of the environment by industry" (they could have been thinking of the pollution of the River Don), "the moulding of consciousness by the media ... the violence of war, and the violence inherent in the ethos of competition; the consistent spectacle of people in authority abusing their privilege for personal gain or proving themselves inadequate for their position".

This large minority group proposed to regard each child as unique. This was the main difference between them and the old guard who liked to marshal pupils in large squads to be drilled. They were questioning the Roman tradition in education. They were trying to envisage how an individual pupil saw his school. They recreated in their minds the conditions in which some children suffered repeated belting. Instead of condemning such a child as a real bad lot, they tried to understand how he (or she) would regard the punitive authority which regulates his (or her) life. The traditionalists diagnosed the situation simply; these children got up in the morning determined to give the teachers hell and therefore must be exposed to an appropriate deterrent. The others saw these pupils as perplexed, reacting instinctively and sometimes fiercely to administrations of pain, lashing out indiscriminately against authority, all authority, because it regarded authority as merely the people licensed to inflict pain. They wanted to "produce in each teacher a constantly expanding awareness of alternative responses which will enable him to define and refine more closely what he considers to be a justified reaction for him. This replaces the simplistic "this is right/this is wrong" approach with a more complex but more realistic knowledge of the issues involved and the possible origins of incidents. It emphasises the uniqueness of each incident with the uniqueness of response which it entails."

There is no young teacher in the country, I believe, who would not feel that this document speaks to his condition. If a doctor fails to cure a patient, he will be sad and disappointed about it, but he will not impute to it a failure of personality as so many teachers (particularly young teachers) do when they feel they are failing in the classroom. The old criterion of teaching was simple. There were "strong" teachers and "weak" teachers. The "strong" teachers got all the pupils in their classroom to be quiet; the "weak" teachers didn't. Once upon a time chemists believed that everything was built out of four elements, earth, air, fire and water, but further analysis showed that matter wasn't all that simple.

As a young teacher I was troubled about this. One day at Kirkcaldy, in Fife, the headmaster brought a senior member of the Scottish Education Department to my classroom and, while we talked, a buzz of conversation grew among the pupils and I felt desolately that if I'd been a "strong" teacher they would have remained obediently and respectfully silent. I was cheered later on to discover that two very distinguished teachers had been initially refused their parchments (a Scottish document attesting to the successful completion of two years of apprenticeship) because they "couldn't keep discipline" and were "weak" teachers. So I say to all teachers, and particularly young teachers, don't be taken in when the old hands try to fix one of these labels on you; if you like children, you'll probably be a good teacher.

But in order to be free to teach in the way you want, you'll have to participate in a much farther-reaching enquiry into the nature of teaching than the old teachers envisaged — something along the lines of this document produced by the younger teachers of Summerhill.

"We should be forming small learning groups on the criteria of social, psychological and emotional need rather than informational need," they wrote. "Discipline, justice, right and wrong cannot be simply codified. Relevance, modification and flexibility are more important than some arbitrary and authoritatively imposed correctness. Although pupils and teachers need some form of security , a code of discipline with specified rules removes personal responsibility from the teacher. How then can we pretend that we are trying to promote personal responsibility in the pupil? Rules protect people from decisions they should be encouraged to make themselves."

I doubt if the staff of any other state school in Scotland has got as far as examining its function in a statement as basic as that. In the hundred years since education became compulsory in Scotland, most of the state teachers have followed the tradition with docility. This docility has been bred into them by schools, churches, parents, newspapers, universities and colleges of education. It is so pervasive, all-embracing, that you don't notice it any more than normally you notice the air until something makes you notice it, such as a hurricane. Here and there in Scottish state schools there is a submerged minority of teachers uneasy at the authoritarianism but discouraged and mostly silent. In Summerhill there was a large minority (but never more than 38). They were asking searching questions about their trade, were dissatisfied with the currently accepted answers and proposed a few answers of their own. That was unusual enough in Scotland to make their statement significant. They had come together from different parts of the world, the product of different cultures and upbringing. But I was relieved that some of them were Scottish.

There was a young geography teacher, a Highland girl whose class gained for Summerhill the first award of a national trophy open to all Scottish secondary schools. Another was a Scottish girl who brought an unusual distinction to the teaching of French and German. They combined enthusiasm and ability with a new attitude of affection for their pupils. What is it that makes some people accept and others question their common upbringing and education? Elizabeth Garrett, deputy head, had received as conventional an education as Aberdeen can provide. She had gone to teach in the Borders, married there, joined Grampian Television as their education officer, and had been responsible for a television programme on sex education which won acclaim throughout the country. Then she returned to teaching as a year mistress in an Aberdeen comprehensive which had been the city's middle-class girls' school. Then she came to Summerhill as deputy head. She worked unobtrusively, a presence and an influence that gave soothing and encouragement to girls in angry revolt. She was on the side of the girls, a rare thing in Scottish education. Some of the more liberal-minded female members of the senior staff in Scottish schools are fair to the disruptive girls but above and outside their lives, like a good judge dispensing equitable justice, dispassionate. She was involved with the pupils. Several times when I assumed a judicial role she intervened with a courteous vehemence to demand, "How would **you** feel if your parents were having a row and you were ill and....?" Now this is the contribution she made to the school, and it is revolutionary. She was not allying herself with the prefecture and striving to manipulate the pupils. She was allying herself with the pupils. And it's the only answer to the problems of education.

Teachers also found support and encouragement from her. A staff room (like an officers' mess) is sometimes a mutual defence society against the common enemy outside, the pupils or the soldiers. It can make life uncomfortable for those teachers who seem to be siding with the pupils. It is this group pressure (which is called gang pressure when it is exerted by pupils) which makes many liberal-minded teachers capitulate to the traditionalists. In these circumstances the minority in the Summerhill staff found comfort in Elizabeth Garrett's support. There are not many senior members of staff in Scotland who are prepared to support teachers who have relinquished the old attitude towards the pupils. Thus she provided a nucleus from which the minority drew strength and survival.

The Director of Education included this minority statement in the envelope of documents he sent out to members of the Education Committee, and ignored it thereafter as far as any public reference was concerned, and the Education Committee gave it little attention.

The envelope of documents the Director of Education sent to the committee members contained the majority statement, histories of disturbed pupils, and a letter I wrote in justification of the work we had done in Summerhill. He had to pronounce on these documents for the guidance of the committee and his advice was included in the envelope. His advice to them had an air of impartiality, but it was the impartiality of a man of conservative educational principles trying to be fair to the other side. His advice spotlights the influence on democratic governments of the permanent officials in central and local government. It's part of the defences of the establishment, a moat manned by administrators in pinstripe trousers waving their umbrellas and shouting, "They shall not pass." On the battlements within the moat we espy the Labour politicians, sorrowfully waving to us to retreat, half aware, some of them, that they are being imprisoned, not defended, by the administrators. It's like a Hollywood epic that has got out of hand.

The director's guidance to the Education Committee concerning these opposed educational philosophies shows where the professional establishment takes its stand in such a confrontation. He said, "In my opinion at this time Summerhill Academy lacks a basic framework of security which can only be provided by an agreed policy of procedures regulating the daily routine of staff and pupils. .... In a community situation, such as a secondary school, there must be recognition of the necessary exercise of authority and acceptance of responsibility — an agreed law and order basis.... Attempts at innovation can be almost counterproductive if they increase unease on the part of the staff. In stating my own views here I am not denying the changing nature of authority, but there must be authority which is recognised." He said that only after decisions were made and implemented on the question of what is permissible and what is not, "can the headmaster and his staff go forward together to deal with the educational issues ... Mr Mackenzie has much to contribute and he can by leadership and positive direction, taking the staff with him, do a great deal for the community that is Summerhill Academy."

I had always found him friendly and indeed sympathetic. He was genuinely a kind man. But these are qualities which a wise establishment looks for in its prefects, qualities which will reassure the doubtful, disarm the critics and gave a general impression of well-being. "Business as usual" is the objective of all establishments. The director hadn't taught for a long time and he was out of touch with the real, urgent nature of an explosive situation. The previous year there had been 75 schoolgirl abortions in the city but I don't think he felt that that fact was relevant to education. Earlier, in a letter to the parents, he had assured them that "a problem exists, the core of which is the behaviour of a minority of pupils who have a disruptive influence on others". It was as easy as that. Deal with the minority and you have solved the problem. He believed that there was nothing in the Summerhill situation which could not be cleared up by sound advice contained in a fair summing up of the situation, a balancing of the pros and cons, an equitable distribution of admonition and compliment. "We're all good chaps together; now go away and get on with the job."

The administrators aren't (and haven't been educated to be) people of flexible mind and buoyant resource who could help to translate ideas into general practice. It's the problem that Crossman described in his Cabinet diaries. This failure isn't entirely due to the conservative sympathies of a large number of administrators in central and local government. It is due also to inertia. They haven't been brought up to feel that this is our world and that we can try to shape it nearer to our heart's desire. They have been educated to believe in the omnipotence of the status quo, and the weakness and fallibility of human endeavour in comparison with this powerful and enduring system. It's a lack of resilience and imagination as much as lack of sympathy. The Aberdeen director was, I'm sure, sensitive to suffering, but during his long tenure of the office, even the younger girls and boys in Aberdeen's primary and secondary schools continued to be hit with leather belts and he didn't let the fact too clumsily obtrude on his consciousness. Similarly-endowed men permitted slavery and the Inquisition and the burning of witches to continue when they might have tried to stop it. Good public relations was the first priority; and in his brief the people who must not be offended were Scotland's three ultra-conservative teachers' unions. The time was not ripe to stop leathering children. The director told me that if I could persuade all the hundred teachers at Summerhill to stop using corporal punishment, he would agree to its abolition. The children would have to wait a long time for that blessed unanimity.

It was part of my educational upbringing to treat with respect statements couched in quiet, reasonable terms. My home upbringing had given me radical sympathies, but as a student I was determined not to be influenced by emotional statements and the prejudice of agitators. I read the editorials in the "quality" papers and was influenced by them — by their reasonable style rather than their factual content, which I had no way of assessing. The director's statement bore the same mark of sweet reasonableness as did these editorials. But on this occasion I did have the background knowledge and I was in a position to assess it. It is not the wise statement it purports to be. It is a superficial statement written by a man in an office in St Nicholas House in Aberdeen who spent his life with circulars and committees and reports. He had little intimate understanding of the turmoil in the lives of some of our children. He and we meant different things by education. The extent of the difference appeared in that statement in which he said that only after decisions had been made about what was permissible and what was not, could the staff and I go forward together to deal with the educational issues. But I thought that **this** was one of the educational issues. I had thought that "in a community situation such as a secondary school" our job was to work out with the pupils how we could live in friendship and harmony together. From our mistakes and successes and experience in this joint endeavour we would learn something of how to conceive a democratic state. But he didn't see education like that. Education for his was transmitting information, and to do that successfully, you had to have a quiet classroom; and to ensure that you had a quiet classroom you told the pupils what they could do and what they couldn't do. A confrontation in which the two sides mean different things by the terms they use (for example "Education") is unlikely to produce fruitful discussion. In the same way some of the editorials slip past our not-critical-enough enquiry by muffling themselves in general terms and avoiding the hard, harsh, identifying outlines, the definition in terms of human experience of the ideas they handle. There is a similar lack of definition in the sentence in which he said that "Mr Mackenzie can by leadership and positive direction, taking the staff with him, do a great deal for the community that is Summerhill Academy". Leadership? What does that mean? I had been accused both of being a dictator and of failing to give a lead. **Positive** direction? Positive means the way in which the established tradition wants you to go. "Taking the staff with him"? The reader would never guess that he had imposed on the school, senior members of staff who were hostile to what we were trying to do.

The official minute of the meeting of the schools' subcommittee, which then discussed these various reports, reported the convener's proposal: "That the subcommittee, being of the opinion that the recommendations contained in the report by the working parties are likely to create an atmosphere and framework conducive to the successful attainment of the aims of the headmaster, resolve to recommend that .... the Education Committee indicate their general approval of the recommendations contained in that report." This was the statement submitted by the staff majority. An amendment was proposed suggesting, among other things, that the Education Committee should not approve the extension of the range of corporal punishment beyond the regulations in force at Summerhill Academy and recognise that there are other means of dealing with anti-social behaviour. The convener's motion got five votes, the amendment got four votes. One of those voting for the convener's motion was a Summerhill teacher who had consistently led the opposition to the changes I had sought to bring about in Summerhill. I had thought he would not take part in a vital discussion and vote in a debate in which he had been so deeply involved, but I was told there was nothing in the regulations to prevent him. When I told a member of the Education Committee that I had been invited to be in attendance during the meeting and had waited throughout the meeting in an anteroom, but had had not been invited to be present at the meeting, he replied that he hadn't been aware that I was available. The Education Committee accepted the advice of the convener's motion. If I had been offered an opportunity to speak, I would have challenged the misrepresentation contained in the wording of the motion. It was saying that the introduction of authoritarian methods were "conducive to the attainment of the aims of the headmaster". In particular the Education Committee were saying that they supported me in seeking to reduce corporal punishment, but the best way to reduce it was, for the present, to increase it.

There followed three months of letters, small meetings, meetings of members of the Education Committee with staff and with parents. The committee convener and a subconvener were much concerned with this problem of leadership. I wouldn't have expected a Labour council to put the emphasis on a "leader". Leadership is a vague term (as undefined as "discipline") which bedevils education. Its meanings vary from "having the confidence to order people to do the things you want them to do" to "having the subtlety to manipulate people into doing things you want them to do, without their noticing". The army and employers are keen on "qualities of leadership"; they are looking for promising "personnel" who will become good N.C.O.s and foremen. The Labour Party has never really thought out the implications of comprehensive education and the result is that the residual ideas of the previous dispensation survive, uninspected. Aberdeen Education Committee were keen that no vital changes should be made in North-East of Scotland education. The convener and subconvener (an Englishman who had achieved the rank of major in the army) said that "firm and effective leadership would have prevented this situation from reaching crisis proportions". I had shown an "inability to be the leader of the team". I had been guilty of "woolly theorising". I had not been "sensitive to staff views".

It seemed to me that they were living in a John Buchan world of smart officers in short, trimmed moustaches issuing crisp orders and receiving instant and unthinking obedience from the soldiery. How can we create a new society, or a system of comprehensive education to prepare for it, when the councillors entrusted with the realisation of comprehensive principles are dominated by ideas from the past, seeing themselves not as soldiers in what Heine called the liberation war of humanity, but officers of the old dispensation? Their idiom, their ways of thinking, their philosophy of life identified them with the old system.

During a meeting of the committee at which they discussed Summerhill and at which I had been invited to be "in attendance" in case I might be called in, I had the opportunity to try and assess the effect of ritual and ceremony and tradition, and what Gray called "the boast of heraldry", on these councillors. I had an hour and a half to wait and that was time to survey the large room into which I had been directed. It contained photographs or pictures of 53 former lord provosts of Aberdeen on the walls. Their varying hairstyles was a comment on the present committee's hostility to long hair. There was the ample wigs of the seventeenth century, the shaggy hairstyles of Victorian times, the short-back-and-sides which lasted right down to the latest picture on the wall. Sir James Taggart, the Lord Provost of 1914-19, whom I remembered opening a wartime fete, had been a granite merchant but for his official photograph he posed as a senior cavalry officer, wearing brown leather leggings and spurs and he had the red band of a staff officer on his hat. I remembered him, thus accoutred,   a pleasant old boy strolling through the marquee and across the grass, at ease with the nobility and perhaps not realising that the leggings and the spurs anu the staff hat and the senior officer rank were the arles by which they had enlisted him in their ranks to serve their interests. A granite merchant in spurs was one of the signs of the times. I looked at his face again and it made on me the impact I remembered from 1915, an open, friendly, one would even say wise, face; probably a successful businessman and a good lord provost. With that bonhommie and bluff wisdom how come he had fallen for all that tinsel? There are gaping chinks in the armour of everybody, by which were accessible. The spurs were his Achilles heel. Reith of the B.B.C. had similarly and about the same year clanked into his father's kirk in Glasgow, wearing spurs. It is tempting to play with the psychology underlying the choice of words; was the motive that "spurred" on these men nothing more than the vanity of showing their fellow citizens that, like knights of old, they had won their spurs?

Is there something of subliminal indoctrination in these phrases? Most heraldry and, I imagine, much symbolism is the tool by which we are fashioned into acceptance of the past's scale of values. At the head of the table in this committee room in which I waited, the seat of the chairman of committee had arm rests and a red back on which was the city's crest, two leopards holding up a shield on which three castles were inscribed; it was a kind of throne. In a corner was a gold-looking spade with which a former lord provost had cut the first sod of a new water system at Cairnton. What would an archaeologist of a thousand years hence make of the spade, the throne, the leopards and the castles? What was in the mind of the people who contrived these things? I try to enter into the thinking processes of the councillors, the mould in which their ideas are cast, the **persona** they have chosen for themselves. They have won commissions in the town council and some are promoted to the House of Commons and the House of Lords. As in France, Labour politics offers as good a ladder as any other activity by which a likely lad can climb up and get a seat in the officers' mess.

In these meetings the Labour conveners had (I believe) no inkling of the revolution in ideas of government on which they had stumbled. The convener was content to give to the staff, as his own opinion, part of the director's summing up given to the Education Committee. The director's minutes of the staff meeting said, "The convener said that the headmaster was responsible for the policy of the school within the general policy of the committee, but that it was a simple matter of realism that he could not implement any policy without the support of the majority of his staff." Was it naivete or calculation that made him forbear to mention that the committee had sometimes selected (out of many applicants) punitive teachers who helped to increase and fortify the majority? But he did admit that the majority document had failed to achieve consensus. The committee proceeded grimly to their further deliberations.

A massive effort was made to persuade parents to attend a meeting with the two conveners and director where the parents would have the opportunity of "indicating views on various aspects of the school which they would wish to bring to the notice of the committee representatives". Most of the 2,000 parents ignored the invitation. Fewer than 200 people, not all of them parents, turned up. Only a small number of those present spoke. As so often in staff meetings and other meetings, most of the hawks were hawklike and spoke; most of the doves were dovelike and didn't. Several speakers did defend the school warmly. But a majority of those who spoke were in favour of corporal punishment and more "discipline". It was enough to persuade the two conveners and the director that they had heard the authentic voice of the people.

There followed a two months' run-in to the finishing post. The director wrote to me: "I must say that you left some doubts in my mind as to your intention to implement all the various recommendations made by the committee as soon as possible. I hope I am mistaken in this impression and, if so, I shall be very pleased to have your assurance to the contrary at an early date."

I found these letters of absorbing interest. I'd often wondered in what terms an establishment sets about its objective of getting a complete, signed recantation from an erring member. The form was simpler than I had expected. There was something almost like a disclaimer of responsibility on the part of the director. "The Education Committee has made a policy decision and expects the appropriate members of its staff to take the necessary action." They awaited a full recantation. Then there would be joy over the repentant sinner and a fresh start.

I was fortunate in having the full support of my wife and family, and deeply grateful. Otherwise I would have had to capitulate. In a situation like this, subtle pressures come into play. I thought bleakly of other teachers without that support, or young teachers setting out on their life's work, who would have been compelled to submit. I wondered how many people have had to capitulate to this cold pressure. This is where the diplomacy ends and the velvet gloves come off. This is where the true nature of the elite is revealed. If all the friendly get-togethers, the courtesy and philosophical talk don't work, out comes the whip. It was a replica of the classroom situation; if the recalcitrant pupil continues in his recalcitrance in spite of prayers and beseechings, out comes the leather belt.

So it's no wonder that they supported the belters in the school; to have given up the belt in their classrooms meant that they would have to renounce force in their dealings with their employees too. And they felt that that wasn't on. But this is the core of our argument. We wanted to renounce the use of force in the school. We believed that force achieves nothing. We believed in human nature, having had much evidence of sheer human goodness snining through twisted experience. But they wouldn't let us, even temporarily as an experiment. It was one small further proof that the governing elite has no intention of relinquishing the use of force. This accumulating evidence is making the people at the receiving end of the system (the pupils, the wage earners, the recalcitrants) become equally insistent on the need for unyielding force, for militancy. We had an opportunity of seeing if the non-violent experiment worked in a microcosm of the troubled western world, and some of our results might have had validity in terms of the adult struggle, the needs of children in a school elucidating the more sophisticated pressures of the adult scene. But the Labour Party wasn't equal to it.

"The Labour Party". That's a term requiring definition. It would be better to say "the majority of the Labour Party" or "the majority of the Labour members of Aberdeen Education Committee". There was a vigorous minority who were out of sympathy with the others. They risked unpopularity in supporting our efforts to decrease corporal punishment. They believed in a more humane school; they stood up for the values which once upon a time were the Labour Party's own values. Throughout the battle they gave us unswerving support in private and in public, and later some of them resigned from the council over this issue, seeing perhaps in their colleagues' opposition to Summerhill a symbol of the Labour Party's changed philosophy. One day, if the Party survives, it will acknowledge its debt to these members who held the line while the rest were trying to broaden the base.

The exchange of letters lasted several weeks. To draw the committee's attention to the punitive spirit of the document which they had accepted and to what this meant in terms of leathering particular children, I wrote about the disturbed homes from which some of the most frequently leathered children came. Their chances of recovering a more stable attitude had been reduced. The director's answer was to ask whose fault it was that the teachers who had belted these pupils didn't know they came from a broken home. (But we couldn't have gone round a hundred teachers telling them about the difficult home backgrounds of some of their pupils. That's another liability of a large school). I quoted the Christian injunction to forgive until seventy times seven, but the director ignored it in his next letter. Our Christian educational system, forever diligent about the inclusion of "religious education" in the curriculum, draws the line at practising inconvenient principles like that. "Christianity — but not too much." Long ago I erupted at these prefects of Christianity as if to say, "For Christ's sake, either you support this Levantine joiner, shouting the odds from his mountain; or you say his gospel won't work." But they wouldn't give an honest yea or nay. I felt then, an incoherent student, that the older people might have some subtle interpretation of Christianity that I might ultimately get round to and agree with. But I know now that it isn't so; they are of the same ilk as their first-century counterparts whom Christ referred to in a devastating metaphor.

The correspondence continued. The director wrote: "I agree with you that the members of the Education Committee were aware of your educational philosophy when you were appointed — and they still are. Nor would I as Director of Education expect you to abandon your educational outlook — although it may be modified by you in the light of experience. This is not the point at issue. What is the concern and responsibility of the committee is to take such action as it deems appropriate to resolve a situation arising from the attempt to translate your aims and objectives into practice at Summerhill Academy. On this the Education Committee had made a decision. I shall be glad to have a reply in terms of the requests made in this and my previous letters."

The exchange of letters was like a game of chess I play with my son when we have reached the stage at which it is only a question of how long it is going to take him to box me up completely. The director's bishops and castles and pawns were closing in.

During this time there was a fair amount of what Matthew Arnold (in **Culture and Anarchy**) described as "a blind clamour against an unpopular personage". Little of the argument of the attack on the schools system, launched by the staff minority, percolated into popular discussion in bus and factory floor. The popular feeling, supported by the churches, was that Summerhill "had no discipline", it was a "place where you could get away with murder", and truths, half-truths, gossip and fabrication were quoted in support of this thesis. All the Aberdeen comprehensives had their troubles, intimidation, vandalism, delinquency, but the sins of Summerhill were highlighted. An observer pointed out that, after much damage was done in another Aberdeen comprehensive and many windows broken, the headmaster was quoted in the local paper in an angry outburst against "this useless, meaningless destruction" and thundered that he would take steps to find the culprits; and this, said the observer, was the required attitude, the ritual response which satisfied the leaders of the community. Nothing about finding the causes. It was a time of vehemence and unreason. One Summerhill teacher described the Education Committee as "an apprehensive (and even frightened) governing institution which refuses to examine fundamental defects in its own system — which are the real sources of conflict".

Outside the state system, the headmaster of Kilquhanity School in Galloway, John Aitkenhead, was getting nearer the truth. He wrote: "The tribulations suffered by hurt kids of all kinds seem to me to lead us to the truth about kids in general. The legislation for approved schools — e.g. no physical or corporal punishment — is away ahead of the normal situation which **forces** kids to come to school and **legalises** adult belting of youngsters. In crude terms that's what our school set-up amounts to: by law they must attend; by law we may knock hell out of them. And it seems to me it's the truants and the non-conformists among the kids who are painfully showing us the truth about ourselves and our stupid assumptions. Like the land maybe; it takes a long time of ill-treating before it revolts and makes us think about what we're doing and have been doing."

In his paper, entitled "Time for Positive Thinking", John Roberts, principal teacher of English at Summerhill, delved below the surface and laid bare the roots of the trouble.

"Any institution needs frequent radical reappraisal because it creates, by its size and complexity, an identity of its own. Certain practices, attitudes and administrative organisations become an accepted part of the fabric — they are unquestioned, often even unnoticed merely because they exist and surround us. This seems to be a good time to step outside Summerhill and assess it objectively but constructively. Few institutions do this because they are frightened about finding skeletons in their cupboards. The general run of schools, education authorities and headmasters leads me to believe that the teachers now at Summerhill will never again be able to participate in such an analysis. 'The first object of those in power is to retain power'.

"We may find, with Marshall McLuhan, that the medium is the message. What our school consists of is not what is taught or the various methods by which it is taught. The values that it expresses are more probably contained in various features of its organisation, hidden and implicit in its structure and therefore hard to identify. The problems we have are not so much evidence that the kids are wrong as manifestations of an anachronistic and increasingly meaningless institution.

"Merely to propose more rules, sanctions and punishments is to increase the restrictive nature of our response to human beings and thereby create repressions much more socially and personally damaging."

His paper went on to express these general ideas in terms of questions about the kind of education which individual children were receiving:

Were the personal and social needs of less privileged children regarded as of less urgency than helping other children to get through their "O" grade and "H" grade external examinations?

(Yes)

Are different learning roles being demanded? Is there an alternation between being expected to talk and being discouraged, between passive assimilation and active initiation?

(Yes)

Would it not be useful to look at a child's output in one week across the curriculum and see what kind of educational process it represented?

(Yes)

Do the concepts and language registers of teachers convert the school into an alien culture for many children? Do teachers in different subjects require different kinds of talk?

(Yes)

He summed it up thus:

"We can take up a defensive posture, concentrating on the mere symptoms of unrest, and invoke the simple and traditional processes of rule-making and restrictions, thus making Summerhill another anonymous school."

Or

"We can take up an innovative posture, considering the sources of unrest, and restructure our system to different priorities, thus placing Summerhill in the vanguard of educational thinking.

"Are we not in grave danger of discarding a great opportunity for positive thinking, and active participation in some of the real educational issues of our time?"

It was ironical that, at the time when Aberdeen Education Committee were turning down a plea like this, parents and people outside schools were questioning the value of hitting their children. "It doesn't work," a parent told me. A **Scotsman** writer pointed out that belting in the Edinburgh schools had hardly lessened since the turn of the century. Scotland had 5,000 people behind bars. "It is our indifference to the state of the nation that makes Scotland a mean and bitter home for many." The committee was buffetted by pressures. The churches felt themselves threatened. A minister of the church who was a committee member said that corporal punishment was a red herring in the Summerhill controversy. The committee was frightened of the teachers' unions. All the unions — Educational Institute of Scotland (46,000 members), the Scottish Secondary Teachers' Association (7,500 members) and the Scottish School-masters' Association (3,000 members) — vigorously supported the teachers' right to belt pupils and opposed any suggestion that a record should be kept of the occasions on which it was used. I don't think that these unions represent teacher opinion any more than, say, the

Church of Scotland represents Scottish opinion, but because they have officially approved structures within the system, an education committee can in part escape responsibility for a decision by suggesting that the decision was forced upon it by these "democratic" institutions. If the Education Committee had supported the Summerhill attempt to reduce corporal punishment, a howl of protest from the official bodies would have menaced their re-election.

I think some of the members of the Education Committee sought refuge in the results of a plebiscite on corporal punishment reported in the Aberdeen Town Council minutes. "The results of a survey of parents' opinions on corporal punishment in primary and special schools were — (A) 8,821 (88.6 per cent) returned. Of these (B) 7.346 (83.28 per cent) wished the present policy continued; (C) 644 (7.30 per cent) wished progressive elimination of corporal punishment; (D) 831 (9.42 per cent) wished immediate abolition."

An Aberdeen sociologist, commenting on these figures, said that the great majority of people are ready to fit in with what seems to them to be intentions of a plebiscite. He said that therefore the results depend on the framing of the questions. They would have got different answers if they had asked, "Would you have any objections if corporal punishment were progressively eliminated?"

But the Education Committee were in no mood to permit the Summerhill experiment to continue. They felt threatened and insecure and, in the words of the convener, longed for a return to "blessed normalcy". The staffing committee which was convened to take "decisive action" recommended my suspension and this recommendation went a few days later to the Education Committee. The convener spoke of "growing concern about the practical aspects of policy implementation at the academy and said there had been a consequential disorientation of approach by the teachers individually and the eventual polarisation by significant numbers of the staff into pro- and anti-Mackenzie groups". He said that when the committee had imposed the staff-majority document on the school I was bound to obey their order to implement it. Because I didn't do so, I had "rendered the exercises of last autumn counterproductive". He concluded his attack with these five points:

"These is no evidence of an acceptable framework of order in the school which is necessary for the ordinary work of the school.

"There is a marked lack of respect between pupils and teachers, pupils and pupils, many teachers and pupils and the headmaster.

"There is confusion about the real meaning of discipline and a false equating of discipline with corporal punishment.

"There is a demonstrable lack of confidence in many parents in the educational provision for their children at Summerhill Academy.

"There is a grave loss of morale among the staff."

After two hours of debate, by a vote of 16 to six, I was suspended from duty, on full pay.

The aftermath was a strange story. The education committee conveyed the impression that, immediately I left it, it was imperative to reintroduce law and order to a school described as chaotic and anarchic, and that was why the Deputy Director of Education, Mr W. U. Henry, was appointed to take over. But only a few days after his arrival he was off on an educational cruise to the Baltic for a fortnight, leaving in charge the deputy head, who was one of my strongest supporters. On his return, he set about dismantling the Summerhill experiment. He knew the history of the Consensus Document and the hundreds of hours that the staff had given to its compilation. I had been suspended because I refused to accept all the provisions of the document. Three months later the document was itself suspended. On 26th June 1974 Mr Henry called a staff meeting. After the meeting he ordered that the final 20 minutes of the staff discussion should be struck from the record. The staff meeting had voted by a majority that the new headmaster would not be bound by the document, would not have to implement it.

The making of a staff document, like the making of a President, shows how democracy is manipulated. Recommendations had been included in it to placate my supporters. One paragraph stated: "When corporal punishment is used, a detailed record should be kept of its use and the reasons for its use." There was no attempt or intention to abide by this decision. When a query was raised, the reply came with a smile: "The document says 'should', not 'must'." Other recommendations had been the setting up of a unit for children with problems, an increase in the number of remedial teachers, staff discussions on primary-secondary liaison, basic standards of communication, school policy and attitudes to education. None of them has happened.

When I was there, the staff insisted on monthly staff meetings. After I left, staff meetings were reduced to one or two a term. These meetings changed, too. They used to be held in the crowded staff room in an informal atmosphere, good for discussion. People sat around in irregular groups. The new headmaster transferred the meetings to the large assembly hall. The staff were drawn up in three rows of seats across the entire width of the hall. New proposals were presented in a formidable manner. The "senior staff" had agreed; the principal teachers had discussed them and agreed. Was there anybody in the hall who now wanted to venture an opinion? No? Fine. Well, that was accepted. Then it would be reported to the staff that in spite of their requests, the classrooms had not been redecorated, no improvements had been made to the burglar alarm system and there was no money available for the flood-lighting of the playground.

Teachers who expressed opinions contrary to the principles of the new regime were accused of being "divisive of staff unity". Fourteen teachers wrote to the Aberdeen daily newspaper recording their dissatisfaction at the increase of corporal punishment in the school. The Director of Education wrote to them, suggesting that they should resign. They were reported to the General Teaching Council for "unprofessional conduct" but, in the end, the case against them was dismissed on a technicality. Different pressures were used on recalcitrant pupils. It is difficult to discover how many suspensions, expulsions and transfers to other schools took place. Official statements of the school's methods of dealing with unwilling pupils said that "harassment" and "persecution" were to be employed. For some months police were called in to the school almost daily. Pupils were belted for forgetting books, for not having pencils, for truancy. Visitors to the school could see a line of pupils waiting to be belted. The local authority had laid it down that only those pupils were to be belted for lateness whose lateness was their own fault. If lateness was the fault of the parent, the pupils were not to be belted. But Summerhill dispensed with such niceties and belted them indiscriminately. Pupils had to get a signed note if they went to the school library, or the lavatory. A regime like this doesn't publish these things and much of what I write is dependent on hearsay. To test the validity of what I wrote, I sent letters to national newspapers making some of these allegations about the school. The letters were published and I waited for a reply from the headmaster or the Director of Education. There was no reply. There haven't been many statements on school policy or educational issues since I left. It's safer that way. At parents' nights a major topic is uniform and the message to the pupils is: "You show pride in your school by wearing uniform; you do not show pride in your school by wearing denim." Education is about denim. Guidance teachers play a much smaller part; the official advice to them is: "Punish first and counsel afterwards." Latin has been introduced. The school cottage beside the Dee is rarely used.

Unlike the new regime, I never believed that a school's main function is to prepare pupils for examinations, although I pointed out to the staff that we owed it to our pupils to help them to gain the certificates which gave them the entry to many walks of life. In gaining these certificates our pupils were reasonably successful. I know from my own figures that the proportion of "O" grade successes when I left was about the same as when I started. Since the new regime took over, the "O" grade examination scores have gone down substantially. Attendance also has deteriorated. Unlike corporal punishment, attendance is a subject for which records are available. A comparison of a randomly chosen week in 1971and 1972 with the same week in 1975 showed a considerable decrease in'75 as far as the pupils of the first three years were concerned. These year-groups were chosen so that the issue would not be complicated by the inclusion of the fourth year pupils unwillingly at school under the Raising of the School Leaving Age Act; but the ROSLA figures for my last year at Summerhill also were better than for the following two years.

Observing from a distance the nature of the methods and their results in the new Summerhill, I see more clearly the philosophy of education that we had in a fumbling way tried to realise. The contrast sharpens and points the lesson to be learned. It's not simply that the new dominies at Summerhill are mindlessly following a tradition, that there is more physical pain, less care for the rejected majority. There is significantly more to it than that. The emphasis is on the drill, the informer, the belt,the uniform, the bowed head,submission, memorising the acceptable information,performing the required rituals, rewards for those who refrain from asking awkward questions. When you look at all these features together, they combine to delineate the dangerous face of authoritarianism.The savage trampling on the nonconformists awakens uncanny echoes, reminders of the battles our Scottish forebears fought against the king and his kirk. Three centuries ago Milton said that the price of liberty is eternal vigilance. It is fought for, and won, and when we are relaxing, the enemies of liberty are prowling back, regrouping, setting one section of our people against the other, to divide and rule. Subtly   (as we enter the last quarter of the twentieth century) they employ the media to preach submission. Callaghan, apparently shifting his ground ever so slightly, has become their mouthpiece. Ideas about the nobility of accepting discipline without question are dribbled into us almost imperceptibly and our critical faculties are dulled. We are entering on dark days. The "Ode to Joy" is postponed. We are a long way from integrating all our people into one society based on a covenant of irreverence and love.

Chapter Seven

A CULTURAL REVOLUTION?

After I was sacked from this job of headmaster, I sat down to write the Summerhill story, introducing it by an analysis of the crisis in Scotland's classrooms. In this final chapter I'd like to link the present crisis with the changing attitudes and beliefs of the community in which I was brought up, and to forecast how further (and now accelerating) changes in attitudes and education may influence the future of Scotland.

I was brought up in a community which believed and accepted. They believed in the kirk and those set in authority over them; they accepted the school and the social order. Some people sometimes asked questions but most were content to accept areas of incomprehensibility as part of the nature of life on earth. There were protests at obvious unfairness or glaring mistakes, but these were only ripples on a smooth loch. People who didn't go to the kirk nevertheless accepted the kirk as part of the structure of their lives. After a hard day's work few people felt like making an analysis of society.

The laird, the doctor, the minister and the dominie (in that order) were the pillars of our rural society. People didn't much question rents, prescriptions, the Trinity, or Latin; these things were part of a mystery. The belief in a Heavenly Father who cared for us and sometimes chastised us for our own good spilled over into terrestrial affairs. Like our Heavenly Father, our earthly rulers were able and willing to help us and we, on our part, acted like good children, obedient, respectful, "well brought up". Parents expected the same recognition from their children as they gave to their rulers. It was a paternalistic society, providing security in exchange for acceptance.

After I left the university I began to have doubts about the picture of our society that the community and school and church and university had given me. Teaching in Germany in 1938 and 1939 I found that professors and churchmen and newspaper editors had discovered that basically they had always been Nazis. When I returned I found the same compliant attitudes towards our own rulers. There was a show of independence, an attempt to suggest that our own professors and churchmen and editors were different from these servile Germans but it was unconvincing. Was that what the Old Testament writer was thinking about when he used the phrase, bowing the knee to Baal?

I read for the first time about the Highland Clearances. They had never been mentioned at Turriff School in Aberdeenshire or in Robert Gordon's College in Aberdeen. A century ago when police from Glasgow and the militia were called in and Skye crofters imprisoned because of a crofters' uprising against their landlords, the local headmaster advised them to respect the law. His granddaughter, who wrote a book about the rising, **The Battle of the Braes**, says that the crofters were quite right to ignore him. When the crofters of Caithness and Sutherland revolted against expropriation in 1854 the Lord Chief Justice said, "All must submit, whatever their feelings, or rank, or perverted notions of right and wrong, to the authority of the law. . . . Neither they nor their neighbours can be allowed to suppose that they can live in this kind of wicked and rebellious spirit against the law. They must be taught submission in the very first instance."

In the R.A.F. I was moved from the sergeants' mess to the officers' mess and wondered what deep natural division separated N.C.O.s from officers, the more especially when Sir Archibald Sinclair, Air Secretary, who was a highland laird, refused to give the same medal to N.C.O.s and officers who had performed the same deeds of gallantry in the same aeroplane; he insisted that the officers should get the D.F.C. and the N.C.O.s the D.F.M. The dominant question in the services was: "Is he officer material?" I wanted to track down this elusive quality and examine it. In a book about whisky, entitled **Scotch**, Sir Robert Bruce Lockhart told the story of James Buchanan who blended and sold the famous whisky called "Black and White". Lockhart described his eyes (well set), his nose (finely chiselled), his chin (firm), his red hair (carefully parted), his eyebrows (bushy), his "beautifully cut frock coat, high single stuck-up collar, pearl‑tiepin, orchid in buttonhole, glossy top hat and malacca cane". And then Lockhart said, "But for slightly prominent ears he could have passed for a blue-blooded aristocrat." In spite of his ears, however, Buchanan was elevated to the peerage. When I returned to teaching after the war I began to ask if the distinction maintained in Scottish schools between the **academic** and the **non-academic** was equally illusory. One unanswered question led to another. Could it be that by the use of words like "officers and other ranks", "academic and non-academic", a minority sought to persuade the majority that they weren't up to the requirements of running their society? There was a Plantagenet Palliser quality still about Westminster, a quality which the new members of the club cultivated rather than sought to dispel.

A North American Indian student visited Summerhill and I learned that North American Indian students were asking questions similar to mine. An American book, **Teaching Multi-cultural Populations**, described one of their student conferences in New Mexico in 1960:

" 'If we organise are we really trying to help our people, or are we going to seek status for ourselves?' " asked Clyde Warrior.

"The Mohawk girl Shirley Wint was troubled by this too: 'Is there any way by which this organisation can guard against political climbing? Can we prevent its being used as a lever to gain high position?'

"The Paiute Mel Thom thought that 'political climbing' was a concept of the white man that was inherent in the structure and goals of his society. It was not tribal nor Indian. Let us organise 'in the Indian way', on the 'high principles derived from the values and beliefs of our ancestors'."

Sympathetic though I was to the Red Indians, I had always believed that they had no wisdom to offer us, that their culture was a pow-wow and wigwam and totem pole affair, picturesque and ineffectual. It took me a long time to see that my education was stage-managed, a deliberate effort to head off any wisdom that might be available from competing cultures. Another incident described in the same book might be regarded as a lesson for western society. An American teacher was puzzled that none of his Navaho pupils ever got two stars for his classroom work. After he'd got one, he stopped competing. An Indian friend explained that Indian children find their security in being a member of a group and not in being singled out and placed in a position above the group. When he learned that, the American teacher took down from the wall the chart on which the gold winners were plotted and the gold stars went on sale cheap. I wondered. Have we in Scotland overdone the gold stars? What magic is there in a C.B.E. that we covet it? What is the nature of the satisfaction that its award gives us?

And that question led to a more general question about what things give real, abiding satisfaction and to doubts about the wildgoose chase after more and more material benefits. Television advertisements and the glossy Sunday supplements entice, seduce, lead you on. With jade necklaces, black candlesticks, suede wallcovering, Jack o' Lantern beckons you as he disappears round the next corner. It's not only the pursuit of the newest accepted elegance; it contains also the deftly turned implication that what you have is old, poor, out-of-taste, dull, peasant-like and that you are of the brutish, peasant type unless you raise yourself out of this condition. What you are at present enjoying is nothing. Here is a coloured picture of so-and-so roasting parakeet at his campfire beside his moored trimaran in a creek in the Galapagos. That, it suggests, is the ultimate in earthly bliss. It is a fugitive Eldorado, this paradise of glossies, and when you finally make it to the creek in the Galapagos and are relaxing, the torture is reimposed and they've got you discontented again. And thus restless, always on the move, never having a moment to spare from the pursuit of Mammon to consider whether there might be other values, deeper satisfactions.

A more general uneasiness, an extension of the anxiety about material things, is infiltrated into us until it becomes our normal frame of mind. We are encouraged to be anxious, diffident, to feel guilty. The schools are responsible for the deliberate cultivation of anxiety in the young. They continually harass their children with thoughts of what will happen to them if they don't get their 'O" grades or Highers, their 'O" levels and "A" levels, three or six years after tomorrow. We parents are guilty if we are not forever on to our children, urging them to keep up in the examination race. We communicate to them our own anxieties about their future. Fear of failure, fear of what will happen to them if they antagonise those who have influence. Children learn to distrust their own abilities and their own natures. They must be always standing on their toes, pretending to be taller than they are, nobler than they are. I was dismayed by the difference between the noble characters in the books I read and my own sinning, ignoble self. Today I see Scottish schools perpetuating this insecurity, and afraid of some of the young who are relaxed and proof against status-seeking.

What dismays me most is the pervasive sense of unreality in our society and in our schools. The kirks don't believe the words they read out on Sundays — take no thought for the morrow; forgive unto seventy times seven; let not your heart be troubled. The politicians don't believe in democracy nor do they bother to define it. Most of the information the schools set such store on is useless, unrelated to the way we live and the way the country is run. I read reports on educational research but they had rarely anything to do with the difficulties I met in the classroom. The media use experts daily to explain economics and finance but millions of us don't understand what they are saying. There is something unnerving about a system of enlightenment that doesn't enlighten. It's like a spectacle of dancers dancing but not to the music the band is playing.

In all ages people had individual doubts about the nature of their society but these doubts have been discouraged by their education, or ridiculed, or lost in the blare of the trumpets, or stifled by the final sanction of the law, and little recorded. They are now rising into consciousness and finding fuller utterance. I learned that I needn't have gone on trying to squeeze my ideas into the accepted pattern, trying to conform. I realised that our society isn't the well-organised-for-us, caring, kindly-father society that I'd been told about and gone on believing in, against the evidence. It's a jungle. It has clearings of caring people here and there, but the pattern isn't one of caring. The people who have power in our society are not usually the servants of a Heavenly Father, able and ready to help us. We have to learn to help ourselves and trust ourselves.

Under the battering of material change and new circumstances of living, our society has to be refashioned. This the priests of the old dispensation are usually unable to do because their training has been largely static, a drilling in the theological, educational and political doctrines and rituals. Confronted by the truths declared by the young, they feel uncomfortably a tacit criticism of themselves for having subjugated themselves to the orthodoxies. They feel the truths they saw when they were young, and denied, returning with (as Emerson puts it) "an alienated majesty". This is the time of transition in ideas. Slowly at first, people begin to change their ground. It is the impact of this change in ideas upon a Scottish comprehensive school that this book seeks to record. As the transition gathers momentum, the old priests, as subject to outbursts of anger as the young heretics, call in chief constables, bishops and newspaper editors to excommunicate them. The going gets rough. It got rough in Summerhill. It is a recurrent story. In **The Outline of History**, H. G. Wells refers to St Dominic who "had a passion for the argumentative conversion of heretics" (we had his reincarnation in Summerhill) and says that the development of St Dominic's Black Friars showed the Roman Church at the parting of the ways, committing itself more and more deeply to organised dogma, and so to a hopeless conflict. "The last discourse of St Dominic to the heretics he had sought to convert is preserved to us. It is a signpost in history. It betrays the fatal exasperation of a man who has lost his faith in the power of truth because **his** truth has not prevailed.

" 'For many years,' he said, 'I have exhorted you in vain, with gentleness, preaching, praying and weeping. But according to the proverb of my country — where blessing can accomplish nothing, blows may avail — we shall rouse against you princes and prelates, who, alas! will arm nations and kingdoms against this land . . . and thus blows will avail where blessings and gentleness have been powerless.' "

In Scottish education the anger of the old priests ran true to the historical form. A year after the Summerhill controversy had reached its climax and I had been dismissed, the Educational Institute of Scotland passed by a large majority a resolution declaring "that this annual general meeting resolves that the Institute should take an active and decisive part in controlling the introduction of new subjects and teaching methods into schools and accordingly instructs Council to prepare proposals whereby major educational innovations could be made only with the approval of subject committees, which would contain a majority of class teachers elected by class teachers''. The Educational Institute of Scotland supported also the Summerhill teachers who refused to keep a record of the occasions on which they used the belt on boys and girls.

An Australian visitor, greeted in the vestibule by a janitor in a peaked cap, would imagine that everything is correct. He would have little inkling of the tragedy of Scottish education, the youngster crying in the lavatory at the pain of the belt on his swollen hand. That's the reality.

What do we teachers do at this stage in a time of transition when the old, failing system assumes the angry measures of St Dominic on the defensive, and backlashes out like a wounded tiger? Many teachers have asked me that question, many of them despondent at seeing the work they have done trampled underfoot and visualising a bleak future in Scottish classrooms. It's important to get this backlash in the historical perspective. Yesterday Smith of Rhodesia was saying that ''not in a thousand years'' would there be black rule in Rhodesia; suddenly he says he has agreed to black rule in two years. It's the bluff of frightened people. As the questions increase, we ask, did Smith really believe that ''not in a thousand years'' . . . or was he kidding? The answer is, he was kidding. So are the Scottish educationists, knowing that their days are numbered. They are unaware of history, having been educated on the reassuring school history books. I dare say that business as usual went on in Rome, amid encouraging noises from the consuls, when the Vandals were sweeping down through Italy. The education committees are unaware of the extent to which change has accelerated. ''Not in a thousand years'' suddenly becomes ''within two years''. If Scotland is wise, it will lay aside its plans for the future on that basis. And it will not be taken in by the peaked hats of the janitors at attention in the vestibule. It will consider the underlying change in attitudes, ideas, determination; the ground swell that determines the waves.

To the teachers I'd say that we should work away quietly, persuading when we can, compromising when we must, trying to speed up the change to a more humane classroom and a more humane society. For example we should support all parents who don't want their children to be flogged in the classroom, informing them about the already available machinery. They should request from the local authority a guarantee that their children should not be physically assaulted by their school teachers. If that guarantee is not forthcoming they should write immediately to Mr A. B. McNulty, Secretary to the European Commission of Human Rights, Council of Europe, Strasbourg 67006, France, simply stating their case and quoting Article 3 of the Convention, and adding a note mentioning Baroness Wooton's and Dennis Canavan's Bills, and their case will be accepted. Also, complaints about child assault by school teachers should be immediately reported to the police and formal charges preferred, and the details sent at the same time to the Scottish Council for Civil Liberties, 214 Clyde Street, Glasgow.

In the vacuum created in Scottish society by the decreasing credibility of politicians of the traditional parties, there is an opportunity for teachers to play a part in the community not envisaged in their old function of filling pupils with exam information. Perhaps the teachers are the best people to resume the dialogue on first and last things which our materialistic masters have neglected. The people of Scotland are coming of age, asking questions about how to use the heritage on which they are entering. Our purpose as teachers is to educate the young so that when they grow up they will be adequately equipped with the understanding to take over their heritage. Like Zimbabwe, Scotland is an emergent nation. The educational controllers of Scotland have no more intention of giving children deep insights into human behaviour and preparing them to grow up to be capable of taking over and running their country than the white settlers in Rhodesia had of preparing black children for a future in which they would run their country. Suddenly it is all changed. The future of Zimbabwe is likely to be different from what the educators planned. The future of Scotland also could be different. In Scotland the forces resisting change are still powerful and, as at Summerhill, determined to maintain control wherever they are challenged. The battle at Summerhill is likely to be repeated in other schools. The result in Scotland could go either way. It's a simple choice for the teachers. Do we agree with Lyward that the key to all deeper insight into human behaviour is not technical proficiency but simply love? If we agree, for the first time in our history the majority of Scottish children could be entering on a cultural revolution.

Reproduced from publishers copy, and printed in Great Britain by
Billing & Sons Ltd, Guildford, London and Worcester